Military Power of the People's Republic of China

A Report to Congress

Pursuant to the National Defense Authorization Act

Fiscal Year 2000

Section 1202, "Annual Report on Military Power of the People's Republic of China," of the National Defense Authorization Act for Fiscal Year 2000, Public Law 106-65, provides that the Secretary of Defense shall submit a report "on the current and future military strategy of the People's Republic of China. The report shall address the current and probable future course of military-technological development on the People's Liberation Army and the tenets and probable development of Chinese grand strategy, security strategy, and military strategy, and of the military organizations and operational concepts, through the next 20 years."

(This page left intentionally blank)

Executive Summary

China's rapid rise as a regional political and economic power with global aspirations is an important element of today's strategic environment – one that has significant implications for the region and the world. The United States welcomes the rise of a peaceful and prosperous China, and it encourages China to participate as a responsible international stakeholder by taking on a greater share of responsibility for the health and success of the global system. However, much uncertainty surrounds the future course China's leaders will set for their country, including in the area of China's expanding military power and how that power might be used.

The People's Liberation Army (PLA) is pursuing comprehensive transformation from a mass army designed for protracted wars of attrition on its territory to one capable of fighting and winning short-duration, high-intensity conflicts against high-tech adversaries – which China refers to as "local wars under conditions of informatization." China's ability to sustain military power at a distance, at present, remains limited but, as noted in the 2006 *Quadrennial Defense Review Report*, it "has the greatest potential to compete militarily with the United States and field disruptive military technologies that could over time offset traditional U.S. military advantages."

China's near-term focus on preparing for military contingencies in the Taiwan Strait, including the possibility of U.S. intervention, appears to be an important driver of its modernization plans. However, analysis of China's military acquisitions and strategic thinking suggests Beijing is also generating capabilities for other regional contingencies, such as conflict over resources or territory.

The pace and scope of China's military transformation has increased in recent years, fueled by continued high rates of investment in its domestic defense and science and technology industries, acquisition of advanced foreign weapons, and far reaching reforms of the armed forces. The expanding military capabilities of China's armed forces are a major factor in changing East Asian military balances; improvements in China's strategic capabilities have ramifications far beyond the Asia Pacific region.

China's strategic forces modernization is enhancing strategic strike capabilities, as evidenced by the DF-31 intercontinental range ballistic missile, which achieved initial threat availability in 2006. China's counterspace program – punctuated by the January 2007 successful test of a direct-ascent, anti-satellite weapon – poses dangers to human space flight and puts at risk the assets of all space faring nations. China's continued pursuit of area denial and anti-access strategies is expanding from the traditional land, air, and sea dimensions of the modern battlefield to include space and cyber-space.

The outside world has limited knowledge of the motivations, decision-making, and key capabilities supporting China's military modernization. China's leaders have yet to explain adequately the purposes or desired end-states of the PLA's expanding military capabilities. China's actions in certain areas increasingly appear inconsistent with its declaratory policies. Actual Chinese defense expenditures remain far above officially disclosed figures. This lack of transparency in China's military affairs will naturally and understandably prompt international responses that hedge against the unknown.

(This page left intentionally blank)

Table of Contents

Figures

Chapter One
Key Developments

"Never before has China been so closely bound up with the rest of the world as it is today."
– China's National Defense in 2006

Several significant developments in China over the past year relate to the questions Congress posed in Section 1202 of the National Defense Authorization Act for Fiscal Year 2000 (P.L. 106-65).

Developments in China's Grand Strategy, Security Strategy, and Military Strategy

- Beijing released *China's National Defense in 2006* in December, its fifth Defense White Paper since 1998, to describe China's security perceptions, national defense policies, and the goals of its modernization programs. As declaratory policy, the paper reflects a modest improvement in transparency, but it does not adequately address the composition of China's military forces, or the purposes and desired end-states of China's military development.

- Beijing released *China's Space Activities in 2006* in October – the previous edition was published in 2000. The paper reviews the history of China's space program and presents a roadmap for the future. The paper also discusses China's cooperation with various partners in space activities. It remains silent on the military applications of China's space programs and counterspace activities.

- In January 2007, China successfully tested a direct-ascent, anti-satellite (ASAT) missile against a Chinese weather satellite, demonstrating China's ability to attack satellites operating in low-Earth orbit. The test put at risk the assets of all space faring nations and posed dangers to human space flight due to the creation of an unprecedented amount of debris.

- Evidence in 2006 suggests that China revised the 1993 *Military Strategic Guidelines for the New Period*, the People's Liberation Army (PLA) guidance documents for military strategy and forces development. The specific contents of the guidelines are not known.

- PRC President Hu Jintao and Russian President Vladimir Putin proclaimed 2006 as "The Year of Russia" during their March meeting in Beijing, the leaders' fifth meeting in less than twelve months. Building on their joint exercise in 2005, the two leaders agreed to increase military exchanges and hold eight cooperative military activities in 2007.

- Reflecting increasing concerns over energy and resource needs, 2006 saw the largest annual increase in new energy contracts signed by China, including new agreements with Saudi Arabia and several African countries. China's effort to court African nations in 2006 culminated with a November summit in Beijing attended by 40 heads of state and delegates from 48 of the 53 African nations.

- In March 2006, China formally launched its 11th Five Year Plan (2006-2010), which includes ambitious calls for a 20 percent reduction in energy consumption per unit of Gross Domestic Product (GDP) by 2010, a doubling of China's 2000 GDP by 2010, and an overall GDP of $4 trillion by 2020. The plan stresses coordinated development, and greater investment and urbanization in the rural interior, to address income disparities and social unrest.

- In 2006, according to the World Bank, China became the world's fourth largest economy, surpassing Great Britain by 0.004 percent in national production as measured by the World Bank's "Atlas" model.

- Official reports claim the number of "mass incidents" declined 22 percent in 2006. Nevertheless, these incidents, directed mainly at local policies and officials, reflect continued popular dissatisfaction with official behavior related to property rights and forced relocations, labor rights, pensions, pollution, corruption, and police brutality.

Developments Related to China's Regional Strategy

- China responded to North Korea's ballistic missile launches over the Sea of Japan in July and nuclear test in October by voting in favor of UN Security Council Resolutions 1695 and 1718 and by continuing efforts to use diplomatic means, specifically the Six Party Talks, which China hosts, to address North Korea's nuclear programs. The Talks, which involve the United States, Japan, South Korea, Russia, and North Korea, as well as China, produced agreement in February 2007 on initial steps to implement the September 2005 Joint Statement on denuclearizing the Korean Peninsula.

- The visit of new Japanese Prime Minister Shinzo Abe to China in November helped to ease somewhat tensions between Tokyo and Beijing. However, issues such as territorial disputes in the East China Sea, over the Senkaku/Diaoyutai islands, and China's efforts to block Japan's quest

for a seat on the UN Security Council remain sources of friction.

- In October 2006, a People's Liberation Army (PLA) Navy SONG-class diesel-electric submarine broached the surface in close proximity to the USS KITTY HAWK aircraft carrier in waters near Japan. This incident demonstrated the importance of long-standing U.S. efforts to improve the safety of U.S. and Chinese military air and maritime assets operating near each other. In 2006, these efforts produced a two phased bilateral search and rescue exercise with the PLA Navy (one phase off the U.S. coast, the second off the PRC coast).

- In 2006, China conducted two counterterrorism exercises with Shanghai Cooperation Organization (SCO) partners, and hosted the fifth anniversary of the founding of the SCO in Shanghai in June.

- China is increasing its role in the Asia-Pacific Economic Cooperation (APEC) group, the Association of Southeast Asian Nations (ASEAN), and the ASEAN Regional Forum (ARF). The United States has encouraged this increased participation, and cooperated with China to co-chair an ARF seminar on non-proliferation. During the October 2006 ASEAN Summit, PRC Premier Wen Jiabao proposed expanded security and defense cooperation between China and ASEAN.

- In November 2006, PRC President Hu Jintao made the first visit to India by a PRC head of state in ten years, demonstrating the importance China places on improving ties with India while preserving its strategic relationship with Pakistan.

Developments in China's Military Forces

China is pursuing long-term, comprehensive transformation of its military forces to improve its capabilities for power projection, anti-access, and area denial. Consistent with a near-term focus on preparing for offensive Taiwan Strait contingencies, China deploys its most advanced systems to the military regions directly opposite Taiwan.

__Ballistic and Cruise Missiles.__ China is developing and testing offensive missiles, forming additional missile units, upgrading qualitatively certain missile systems, and developing methods to counter ballistic missile defenses.

- By October 2006, China had deployed roughly 900 mobile CSS-6 and CSS-7 short-range ballistic missiles to garrisons opposite Taiwan, expanding at a rate of more than 100 missiles per year. Newer versions of these missiles have improved range and accuracy.

- China is modernizing its longer-range ballistic missile force by adding more survivable systems. The road-mobile, solid-propellant DF-31 intercontinental-range ballistic missile (ICBM) achieved initial threat availability in 2006 and will likely achieve operational status in the near future, if it has not already done so. A longer range variant, the DF-31A, is expected to reach initial operational capability (IOC) in 2007. China is also working on a new submarine-launched ballistic missile, the JL-2 (IOC 2007-2010), for deployment on a new JIN-class (Type 094) nuclear-powered ballistic missile submarine, also in development.

- China continues to explore the use of ballistic and cruise missiles for anti-access missions, including counter-carrier and land attack, and is working on reconnaissance and communication systems to improve command, control, and targeting.

__Naval Power.__ China's naval forces include 72 principal combatants, some 58 attack submarines, about 50 medium and heavy amphibious lift vessels, and approximately 41 coastal missile patrol craft.

- China received the second of two Russian-made SOVREMENNYY II guided missile destroyers (DDG) in late 2006. These DDGs are fitted with anti-ship cruise missiles (ASCMs) and wide-area air defense systems that feature qualitative improvements over the earlier SOVREMENNYY-class DDGs China purchased from Russia.

- China is building and testing second-generation nuclear submarines with the JIN-class (Type 094) nuclear-powered ballistic missile submarine and the SHANG-class (Type 093) nuclear-powered attack submarine, which began sea trials in 2005.

- China took delivery of two KILO-class submarines from Russia, completing a contract for eight signed in 2002. China operates twelve KILOs, the newest of which are equipped with the supersonic SS-N-27B ASCM, and wire-guided and wake-homing torpedoes.

- The PLA Navy's newest ship, the LUZHOU-class (Type 051C) DDG is designed for anti-air warfare. It will be equipped with the Russian SA-N-20 SAM system controlled by the TOMBSTONE phased-array radar. The SA-N-20 more than doubles the range of current PLA Navy air defense systems marking a significant improvement in China's ship-borne air defense capability.

- The LUZHOU-class DDG complements ongoing developments of the LUYANG I (Type 052B) and LUYANG II (Type 052C) DDGs. The LUYANG I is fitted with the Russian SA-N-7B GRIZZLY

SAM and the YJ-83 ASCM. The LUYANG II is fitted with an air defense system based on the indigenous HHQ-9 SAM.

- In 2006, China began producing its first guided-missile frigate (FFG), the JIANGKAI II (Type 054A). The JIANGKAI II will be fitted with the medium range HHQ-16, a vertically launched naval surface-to-air missile currently in development.

- At the 2006 Zhuhai Air Show, PRC military and civilian officials asserted China's interest in building an aircraft carrier.

Air Power. China has more than 700 combat aircraft based within an un-refueled operational range of Taiwan and the airfield capacity to expand that number significantly. Many aircraft in the PLA force structure are upgrades of older models (e.g., re-engined B-6 bombers for extended ranges); however, newer aircraft make up a growing percentage of the inventory.

- The PLA Air Force (PLAAF) is deploying the F-10 multi-role fighter to operational units. The F-10, a fourth generation aircraft, will be China's premier fighter in the coming decades.

- China is now producing the multi-role Su-27SMK/FLANKER (F-11A) fighter under a licensed co-production agreement with Russia following an initial production run of Su-27SKs (F-11). China is employing increasing numbers of the multi-role Su-30MKK/FLANKER fighter-bomber and its naval variant, the Su-30MK2.

- Chinese aircraft are armed with an increasingly sophisticated array of air-to-air and air-to-surface weapons, satellite and laser-guided precision munitions, and cruise missiles.

- China's first indigenously produced attack helicopter, the Z-10, is undergoing flight testing. The Z-10 will fire the Red Arrow 8E anti-tank guided missile, offering combat performance equal to the Eurocopter Tiger, but below that of the AH-64 Apache.

- Improvements to the FB-7 fighter program will enable this older aircraft to perform nighttime maritime strike operations and use improved weapons such as the Kh-31P (AS-17) anti-radiation missile and KAB-500 laser-guided munitions.

Air Defense. In the next few years, China will receive its first battalion of Russian-made S-300PMU-2 surface-to-air missile systems. With an advertised intercept range of 200 km, the S-300PMU-2 provides increased lethality against tactical ballistic missiles and more effective electronic countermeasures. China also is developing the indigenous HQ-9 air defense missile system, a phased array radar-based SAM with a 150 km range. As noted above, a naval variant (HHQ-9) will deploy on the LUYANG II DDG and a vertical launch naval SAM (HHQ-16) will deploy on the JIANGKAI II FFG.

Ground Forces. China has about 1.4 million ground forces personnel with approximately 400,000 deployed to the three military regions opposite Taiwan. China has been upgrading these units with tanks, armored personnel carriers, and additional artillery pieces. In April 2006, China made its first delivery of the new third generation main battle tank, the ZTZ-99, to units in the Beijing and Shenyang military regions.

Amphibious Forces. The PLA has deployed a new amphibious assault vehicle (AAV) and developed a range of modifications for existing vehicles including flotation tanks and mounted outboard engines. Its newer amphibious vehicles have greater stability and performance in open water. Increased amphibious training, including multiple training evolutions in a single year, is building proficiency among China's amphibious forces.

Developments in Chinese Military Doctrine

- China continues to focus on capabilities to operate under "informatized" conditions with an emphasis on integrated joint operations, joint logistics, and long-range mobility.

- In June 2006, the PLA released new guidance to increase realism in training and to expand the use of simulators and opposing forces in training evolutions.

- In December 2006, the leaders of the command colleges for the PLA Second Artillery Corps, the PLA Navy, PLA Air Force, and PLA ground forces signed a cooperative education agreement paving the way for joint professional military education.

- In December 2006, the National Defense Mobilization Committee issued the "Outline of National Defense Education for all Citizens," to standardize defense education across China. The goals of such education include "arousing patriotism … and raising the citizens' awareness of their national defense duty."

Assessment of Challenges to Taiwan's Deterrent Forces

There were no armed incidents in the vicinity of the Taiwan Strait in 2006 and the overall situation remained stable, as it was for most of 2005. Beijing reacted responsibly to Taiwan President Chen Shui-bian's decision to suspend the National Unification Council and National Unification Guidelines in early 2006. However, China's military modernization and the deployment of advanced capabilities opposite the island have not eased, with the balance of forces continuing to shift in the mainland's favor. Tension could also increase as Taiwan prepares for its next presidential election planned for March 2008.

- Taiwan appears to be reversing the trend of declining defense expenditures. In 2005, Taiwan leaders announced plans to increase defense spending to three percent of GDP by 2008. In 2006, this figure was approximately 2.4 percent of GDP. The 2007 defense budget requests funds at a level of 2.8 percent of GDP, with a planned 2007 supplemental request expected to raise this figure to 2.85 percent.

- Taiwan abandoned the strategy of using a Special Budget to procure major defense systems approved for sale by the United States in 2001. It will attempt instead to fund the programs in the regular defense budget and budget supplementals. Taiwan's Legislative Yuan has yet to pass these funding bills, however.

- Consistent with the provisions of the Taiwan Relations Act, Public Law 96-8 (1979), the United States continues to make available defense articles, services, and training assistance to enable Taiwan to maintain a sufficient self-defense capability. In September 2006, Taiwan accepted delivery of the last two of four KIDD-class DDGs.

Chapter Two
Understanding China's Strategy

"冷静观察, 站稳脚跟, 沉着应付, 韬光养晦, 善于守拙, 绝不当头."

"Observe calmly; secure our position; cope with affairs calmly; hide our capacities and bide our time; be good at maintaining a low profile; and never claim leadership."

– Deng Xiaoping's "24 Character Strategy

Overview

China's leaders do not explicitly provide an overarching "grand strategy" that outlines strategic goals and the means to achieve them. Such vagueness may reflect a deliberate effort to conceal strategic planning, as well as uncertainties, disagreements, and debates that China's leaders themselves have about their own long-term goals and strategies. Still, it is possible to make some generalizations about Chinese "grand strategy" based on strategic tradition, historical patterns, statements and official papers, an emphasis on certain military capabilities, and recent diplomatic efforts.

Strategy with Chinese Characteristics

At the core of China's overall strategy rests the desire to maintain the continuous rule of the Chinese Communist Party (CCP). A deep-rooted fear of losing political power shapes the leadership's strategic outlook and drives many of its choices. As a substitute for the failure of communist ideology, the CCP has based its legitimacy on the twin pillars of economic performance and nationalism. As a consequence, domestic economic and social difficulties may lead China to attempt to bolster support by stimulating nationalist sentiment which could result in more aggressive behavior in foreign and security affairs than we might otherwise expect.

Chinese leaders and strategists rarely use a Western "ends-ways-means" construct to discuss strategy. Rather, they discuss strategy in terms of two central concepts: "comprehensive national power" (CNP) and the "strategic configuration of power." These concepts shape how Chinese strategic planners assess the security environment, gauge China's relative position in the world, and make adjustments to account for prevailing geopolitical trends.

CNP. China's strategic planners use CNP scores to evaluate China's standing in relation to other nations. These scores are based on qualitative and quantitative measures of territory, natural resources, economic prosperity, diplomatic influence, international prestige, domestic cohesiveness, military capability, and cultural influence. China's leading civilian and military think tanks apply slightly different criteria for CNP. A 2006 report by the Chinese Academy of Social Sciences, for example, used economic, military, and diplomatic metrics to rank China sixth among the world powers.

Since the early 1980s, China's leaders have described their national development strategy as a quest to increase China's CNP. They stress economic growth and innovation in science and technology as central to strengthening CNP. A

The "24 Character" Strategy

In the early 1990s, former paramount leader Deng Xiaoping (d. 1997) gave guidance to China's foreign and security policy apparatus that, collectively, has come to be known as the "24 character" strategy: *"observe calmly; secure our position; cope with affairs calmly; hide our capacities and bide our time; be good at maintaining a low profile; and never claim leadership."* Later, the phrase, "make some contributions (*you suo zuo wei*)" was added.

Elements of this strategy have often been quoted by senior Chinese national security officials and academics, especially in the context of China's diplomacy and military strategy. Certain aspects of this strategy have been debated in recent years – namely the relative emphasis placed upon "never claim leadership" or "make some contributions." China's increased international profile, especially since the 2002 16th Party Congress, suggests Beijing is leaning toward a more assertive, confident diplomacy. Taken as a whole, Deng's strategy remains instructive in that it suggests both a short-term desire to downplay China's capabilities and avoid confrontation, and a long-term strategy to build up China's power to maximize options for the future.

key assumption of this strategy is that economic prosperity and stability will afford China greater international influence and diplomatic leverage as well as a robust, modern military.

A commentary in the official *Liberation Army Daily* in April 2006 shed some light on the relationship between CNP, military modernization, and China's international status: "As China's comprehensive strength is incrementally mounting and her status keeps on going up in international affairs, it is a matter of great importance to strive to construct a military force that is commensurate with China's status and up to the job of defending the interests of China's development, so as to entrench China's international status."

<u>*"Strategic Configuration of Power."*</u> The "strategic configuration of power," or *"shi,"* is roughly understood as an "alignment of forces," although there is no direct Western equivalent to the term. Chinese strategic planners continuously assess the "strategic configuration of power" for potential threats (e.g., potential conflict over Taiwan that involves the United States) as well as opportunities

(e.g., the collapse of the Soviet Union) that might prompt an adjustment in national strategy.

China's leaders describe the initial decades of the 21st Century as a "20-year period of opportunity," meaning that regional and international conditions will generally be peaceful and conducive to economic, diplomatic, and military development and thus to China's rise as a great power. Closely linked to this concept is the "peaceful development" campaign to assuage foreign concerns over China's military modernization and its global agenda by proclaiming that China's rise will be peaceful and that conflict is not a necessary corollary to the emergence of a new power.

Stability, Sovereignty, and Strategy

The perpetuation of CCP rule shapes Beijing's perceptions of China's domestic political situation and the international environment. Regime survival likewise shapes how Party leaders view instability along China's periphery – e.g., North Korea, Central Asia – which could escalate or spill over into China. Concern over maintaining legitimacy also influences how Beijing treats the status of China's land and maritime territorial claims, since any challenge to Chinese sovereignty could undermine the strength and authority of the Party.

China has settled territorial disputes with many of its neighbors in recent years. However, disputes with Japan in the East China Sea, with India along their shared border, and with Southeast Asian nations in the South China Sea remain. Although China has attempted to prevent these disputes from disrupting regional relations, occasional statements by PRC officials underscore China's resolve in these areas. For example, on the eve of President Hu's historic October 2006 visit to India, PRC Ambassador Sun Yuxi told Indian press, "the whole of what you call the state of Arunachal Pradesh is Chinese territory . . . we are claiming all of that – that's our position."

Balance, Position, and Strategy

Beyond China's efforts to maintain stability on its borders and assert its territorial claims, Beijing seeks to advance its strategic interests into the "greater periphery" encompassing Central Asia and the Middle East. The security goals behind this emphasis include maintaining access to resources and markets, and establishing a regional presence and influence to balance and compete with other powers, including the United States, Japan, and India in areas distant from China's borders.

Similarly, China's strategy for the developing world seeks to secure access to resources and markets, build influence in multilateral bodies such as the United Nations, and restrict Taiwan's diplomatic space. To build these relationships, China emphasizes its self-proclaimed status as the leader of the developing world and one that can sympathize with local dissatisfaction over the effects of globalization and perceptions of a widening "north-south" gap.

Resource Demands and Strategy

As China's economy grows, dependence on secure access to markets and natural resources, particularly metals and fossil fuels, is becoming a more urgent influence on China's strategic behavior. At present, China can neither protect its foreign energy supplies nor the routes on which they travel, including the Straits of Malacca through which some 80 percent of China's cruse oil imports transit – a vulnerability President Hu refers to as the "Malacca Dilemma."

China relies on coal for some two-thirds of its energy, but its demand for oil and gas is increasing. In 2003, China became the world's second largest consumer and third largest importer of oil. China currently imports over 40 percent of its oil (about 2.5 million barrels per day in 2005). By 2025, this figure could rise to 80 percent (9.5 – 15 million barrels per day). China began filling a strategic petroleum reserve in 2006. By 2015, Beijing plans to build reserves to the International Energy Agency standard of 90-days supply, but with poor logistics and transportation networks, this may still prove inadequate.

Nuclear power and natural gas account for smaller, but growing, portions of energy consumption. China plans to increase natural gas utilization from 3 percent to 8 percent of total consumption by 2010. Similarly, China plans to build some 30 1,000-megawatt nuclear power reactors by 2020.

China's reliance on foreign energy imports has affected its strategy and policy in significant ways. It has pursued long-term energy supply agreements in Angola, Central Asia, Chad, Egypt, Indonesia, Iran, Nigeria, Oman, Russia, Saudi Arabia, Sudan, and Venezuela. China has used economic aid, diplomatic favors, and, in some cases, the sale of

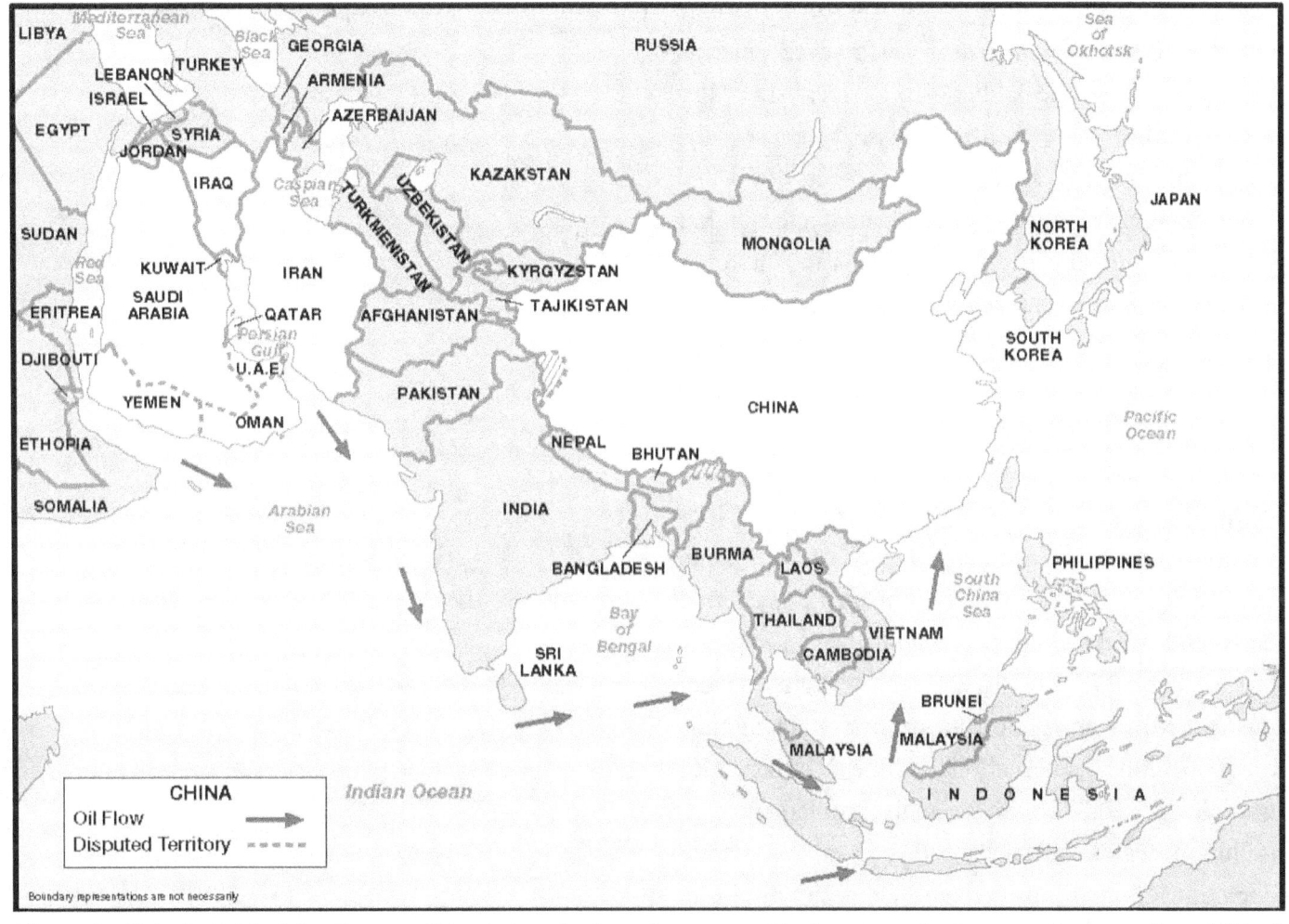

Figure 1. China's Critical Sea Lanes. *China is heavily dependent upon critical sea lanes for its energy imports. Some 80% of China's crude oil imports transit the Straits of Malacca.*

military technology to secure energy deals. China's desire to meet its energy needs, moreover, has led it to strengthen ties with countries that defy international norms on issues ranging from human rights, support for international terrorism, and proliferation.

In the past few years, China has also offered economic assistance and military cooperation with countries located astride key maritime transit routes. Concern over these routes has also prompted China to pursue maritime capabilities that would help it ensure the safe passage of resources through international waterways.

Other Factors Influencing Chinese Strategy

Economic Reform. Economic success is central to China's emergence as a regional and global power, and is the basis for an increasingly capable military. However, underlying structural weaknesses threaten economic growth. Demographic shifts and social dislocations are stressing an already weak social welfare system. Economic setbacks or downturns could lead to internal unrest, potentially giving rise to greater reliance on nationalism to maintain popular support.

Political Reform. In an October 2005 White Paper on Political Democracy, China's leaders reaffirmed the "people's democratic dictatorship," and declared that China is "against the anarchic call for 'democracy for all.'" However, internal pressures for political liberalization persist. Party leaders criminalize political dissent, censor the media and internet, suppress independent trade and labor unions, repress ethnic Tibetan and Uighur minorities, and harass religious groups and churches not recognized by the regime. The Party is wary of any unsanctioned organization in China, even if non-political, fearing these organizations could facilitate organized opposition.

Non-Traditional Security Challenges. Non-traditional security challenges such as epidemic disease (e.g., HIV, avian influenza), systemic corruption (according to official Chinese press, more than 17,500 government officials were prosecuted for corruption in the first eight months of 2006 alone), international crime and narcotics trafficking, and environmental problems (e.g., pollution, water shortages, and renewable resource depletion) could exacerbate Chinese domestic unrest and serve as sources of regional tension and instability.

Chapter Three
China's Military Strategy and Doctrine

". . . resolutely and effectively carry out the sacred duty of defending national sovereignty, unification, territorial integrity, and security . . ."

– Hu Jintao

Overview

Chinese military theorists have developed a framework for doctrine-driven reform to build a force capable of fighting and winning "local wars under conditions of informatization." This concept emphasizes the role of modern information technology as a force-multiplier enabling the PLA to conduct military operations with precision at greater distances from China's borders. Drawing upon lessons learned from foreign conflicts, particularly U.S.-led campaigns up to and including Operation ENDURING FREEDOM and Operation IRAQI FREEDOM, Soviet and Russian military theory, and the PLA's own, albeit limited, combat history, Chinese military planners are pursuing transformation across the whole of China's armed forces.

The pace and scale of these reforms is impressive; however, the PLA remains untested in modern warfare. This lack of operational experience complicates outside assessment of the PLA's progress in meeting the aspirations of its doctrine. The same applies to internal assessment and decision-making among China's senior civilian leaders who, for the most part, lack direct military experience, giving rise to a greater potential for miscalculations in crises. Such miscalculations would be equally catastrophic whether based on advice from operationally inexperienced commanders or from "scientific" combat models divorced from the realities of the modern battlefield.

Military Strategic Guidelines

China does not publish an equivalent to the U.S. *National Military Strategy*. Outside observers therefore have few direct insights into the leadership's thinking about the use of force or into the contingencies that shape the PLA's force structure or doctrine. Analysis of authoritative speeches and documents suggests China relies on a body of overall principles and guidance known as "Military Strategic Guidelines" to plan and manage the development and use of the armed forces.

The PLA has not made the contents of the "guidelines" available for outside scrutiny. Scholarly research suggests that the current "guidelines" most likely date to 1993, reflecting the impact the 1991 Persian Gulf War and the collapse of the Soviet Union had on PRC military-strategic thinking, forming the basis for much of the PLA's transformation over the past decade. However, speeches, authoritative commentary, and new military training guidance suggest that some elements of the 1993 "guidelines" may have been revised recently. These revisions appear to reflect China's perceptions of its security environment and the character of modern war (i.e. "local wars under conditions of informatization"), progress in and lessons learned from China's military modernization, a shift from "building" forces for modern, information-age warfare to training to "win" such wars, as well as Hu Jintao's own ideological imprimatur.

The operational, or "active defense," component of the "guidelines," appears to remain intact. The "active defense" posits a defensive military strategy in which China does not initiate wars or fight wars of aggression, but engages in war only to defend national sovereignty and territorial integrity.

Beijing's definition of an attack against its sovereignty or territory is vague, however. The history of modern Chinese warfare is replete with cases in which China's leaders have claimed military preemption as a strategically defensive act. For example, China refers to its intervention in the Korean War (1950-1953) as the War to Resist the United States and Aid Korea. Similarly, authoritative texts refer to border conflicts against India (1962), the Soviet Union (1969), and Vietnam (1979) as "Self-Defense Counter Attacks." This logic suggests the potential for China to engage in military preemption, perhaps far from its borders, if the use of force protects or advances core interests, including territorial claims (e.g., Taiwan and unresolved border or maritime claims).

Once hostilities have begun, according to the PLA text, *Science of Campaigns (Zhanyixue)* (2000), "the essence of [active defense] *is to take the*

Is China Developing A Preemptive Strategy?

Over the past decade, as the PLA transformed from an infantry-dominated force with limited power projection ability into a more modern force with long-range precision strike assets, China acquired weapon systems and adopted operational concepts that enable military preemption (including surprise attack) along its periphery.

- As of October 2006, the PLA 2nd Artillery Corps had roughly 900 short-range ballistic missiles in its inventory. Acquisition of Su-30 strike aircraft and the F-10 fighter aircraft – both of which are equipped with a variety of precision guided munitions – has improved China's offensive air power. The PLA is also building capabilities for information warfare, computer network operations, and electronic warfare, all of which could be used in preemptive attacks.

- PLA authors describe preemption as necessary and logical when confronting a more powerful enemy. Chinese doctrinal materials stress that static defenses are insufficient to defend territory based on the speed and destructive power of modern forces. As a result, PLA operational concepts seek to prevent enemy forces from massing and to keep the enemy off balance by seizing the initiative with offensive strikes. According to PLA theorists, an effective defense includes destroying enemy capabilities on enemy territory before they can be employed.

China's acquisition of power projection assets, including long-distance military communication systems, airborne command, control, and communications aircraft, long-endurance submarines, unmanned combat aerial vehicles (UCAVs), and additional precision-guided air-to-ground missiles indicate that the PLA is generating a greater capacity for military preemption. PLA training that focuses on "no-notice," long-range strike training or coordinated air/naval strikes against groups of enemy naval vessels could also indicate planning for preemptive military options in advance of regional crises.

---

initiative and to annihilate the enemy . . . . While strategically the guideline is active defense, [in military campaigns] the emphasis is placed on taking the initiative in active offense. Only in this way can the strategic objective of active defense be realized" (emphasis added).

In addition to developing the capacity to annihilate opposing forces, the PLA is exploring options for limited uses of force. Chinese campaign theory defines these options as "non-war" uses of force – an extension of political coercion and not full-scale acts of war. The 1995 and 1996 amphibious exercises and missile firings in the Taiwan Strait are examples of "non-war" uses of force. However, the concept also includes air and missile strikes, assassinations, and sabotage. Such writings highlight the potential for China to miscalculate, given the likelihood that the target of any such actions, if not the broader international community, would view them as acts of war.

Asymmetric Warfare

Identifying and exploiting asymmetries is a fundamental aspect of Chinese strategic and military thinking, particularly as a means for a weaker force to defeat one that is stronger. Since the 1991 Persian Gulf War and Operation ALLIED FORCE, Chinese military strategists have emphasized using asymmetric approaches to exploit vulnerabilities of technologically superior opponents. A 1999 *Liberation Army Daily* editorial suggested this explicitly: "a strong enemy with absolute superiority is certainly not without weakness that can be exploited by a weaker side. ...[O]ur military preparations need to be more directly aimed at finding tactics to exploit the weaknesses of a strong enemy." Elements of China's exploration of asymmetric warfare options can be seen in its heavy investment in ballistic and cruise missile systems, including advanced anti-ship cruise missiles; undersea warfare systems, including submarines and advanced naval mines; counterspace systems;

A Comprehensive View of Warfare

Over the past two decades, Chinese civilian and military strategists have debated the nature of modern warfare. These debates draw on sources within the Chinese strategic tradition and its historical experiences to provide perspective on the "revolution in military affairs," "asymmetric warfare," and "informatized" war. Such debates highlight China's interest in non-kinetic means of warfare and the increased role of economic, financial, information, legal, and psychological instruments in Chinese war planning. Underscoring the PRC military's comprehensive, multi-dimensional view of warfare, the PLA Academy of Military Science text, the *Science of Military Strategy* (2000), notes that "war is not only a military struggle, but also a comprehensive contest on fronts of politics, economy, diplomacy, and law."

Recently, PRC military strategists have taken an increasing interest in international law as an instrument to deter adversaries prior to combat. In a Taiwan Strait context, China could deploy an information campaign to portray third-party intervention as illegitimate under international law. China is also attempting to shape international opinion in favor of a distorted interpretation of the UN Convention on the Law of the Sea by moving scholarly opinion and national perspectives away from long-accepted norms of freedom of navigation and toward interpretations of increased sovereign authority over the 200 nautical mile Exclusive Economic Zone, the airspace above it, and possibly outer space.

computer network operations; and, special operations forces.

The Role of Secrecy and Deception in Chinese Military Strategy

The stress on seizing the initiative in conflicts and keeping the adversary off balance in Chinese military strategy gives rise to a strong emphasis on deception at the strategic, operational, and tactical levels. Chinese doctrinal materials define strategic deception as "[luring] the other side into developing misperceptions . . . and [establishing for oneself] a strategically advantageous position by producing various kinds of false phenomena in an organized and planned manner with the smallest cost in manpower and materials."

In addition to information operations and conventional camouflage, concealment, and deception, the PLA draws from China's historical experience and the traditional roles that stratagem and deception have played in Chinese statecraft. Recent decades have witnessed within the PLA a resurgence of the study of classic Chinese military figures Sun-tzu, Sun Pin, Wu Ch'i, and Shang Yang and their writings, all of which contain precepts on the use of deception.

The Chinese Communist Party's heavy reliance on secrecy acts in tandem with military deception to limit transparency in national security decision-making, military capabilities, and strategic intentions. However, over-confidence may result from military leaders enamored with the uncertain benefits of stratagem and deception. In addition, the same skills commanders use against adversaries can be used to cover up or slow the transmission of bad news internal to the PLA system, a chronic problem in the PRC. Secrecy and deception may therefore be a double-edged sword, confusing China's leaders as much as China's adversaries.

Chapter Four
Force Modernization Goals and Trends

"China pursues a three-step development strategy in modernizing its national defense . . . . The first step is to lay a solid foundation by 2010, the second is to make major progress around 2020, and the third is to basically reach the strategic goal of building informatized armed forces and being capable of winning informatized wars by the mid-21st century."

— China's National Defense in 2006

Overview

China's leaders have stated their intentions and allocated resources to pursue broad-based military transformation to enable joint operations that encompasses force-wide professionalization; improved training; more robust, realistic joint exercises; and accelerated acquisition of modern weapons. For the moment, China's military is focused on assuring the capability to prevent Taiwan independence and, if Beijing were to decide to adopt such an approach, to compel the island to negotiate a settlement on Beijing's terms. At the same time, China is laying the foundation for a force able to accomplish broader regional and global objectives.

The Intelligence Community estimates China will take until the end of this decade or later to produce a modern force capable of defeating a moderate-size adversary. In building such a capability, China's leaders stress asymmetric strategies to leverage China's advantages while exploiting the perceived vulnerabilities of potential opponents using so-called Assassin's Mace programs. The January 2007 ASAT test could be viewed in this context.

The PLA's ambition to conduct joint operations can be traced to lessons learned from U.S. and Coalition operations since the 1991 Persian Gulf War. Since 2004, the PLA has conducted a number of exercises designed to develop the PLA's joint operational concepts and demonstrate new capabilities, command automation systems, and weapons. The PLA hopes eventually to fuse service-level capabilities with an integrated network for command, control, communications, computers, intelligence, surveillance, and reconnaissance (C4ISR), a new command structure, and a joint logistics system. However, it continues to face deficiencies in inter-service cooperation and actual experience in joint operations.

As PLA modernization progresses, twin misperceptions could lead to miscalculation or crisis. First, other countries may underestimate the extent to which Chinese forces have improved. Second, China's leaders may overestimate the proficiency of their forces by assuming new systems are fully operational, adeptly operated, adequately maintained, and well integrated with existing or other new capabilities.

Emerging Area Denial/Anti-Access Capabilities

In the near term, China is prioritizing measures to deter or counter third-party intervention in any future cross-Strait crises. China's approach to dealing with this challenge centers on what DoD's 2006 *Quadrennial Defense Review* report refers to as disruptive capabilities: forces and operational concepts aimed at preventing an adversary from deploying military forces to forward operating locations, and/or rapidly destabilizing critical military balances. In this context, the PLA appears engaged in a sustained effort to develop the capability to interdict, at long ranges, aircraft carrier and expeditionary strike groups that might deploy to the western Pacific. Increasingly, China's area denial/anti-access forces overlap, providing multiple layers of offensive systems, utilizing the sea, air, and space.

PLA planners have observed the primacy of precision strike in modern warfare and are investing in offensive and defensive elements of this emerging regime. China is pursuing improved ISR assets ranging from unmanned aerial vehicles, satellite constellations, and "informatized" special operations forces which could provide targeting data for long-range precision strikes when linked with robust communications. The PLA envisions precision strike capabilities sufficient to hold at risk

western Pacific airbases, ports, surface combatants, land and space-based C4ISR, air defense systems, and command facilities.

To prevent deployment of naval forces into western Pacific waters, PLA planners are focused on targeting surface ships at long ranges. Analyses of current and projected force structure improvements suggest that in the near term, China is seeking the capacity to hold surface ships at risk through a layered defense that reaches out to the "second island chain" (i.e., the islands extending south and east from Japan, to and beyond Guam in the western Pacific Ocean). One area of apparent investment emphasis involves a combination of medium-range ballistic missiles, C4ISR for geo-location of targets, and onboard guidance systems for terminal homing to strike surface ships on the high seas or their onshore support infrastructure. This capability would have particular significance, owing to the

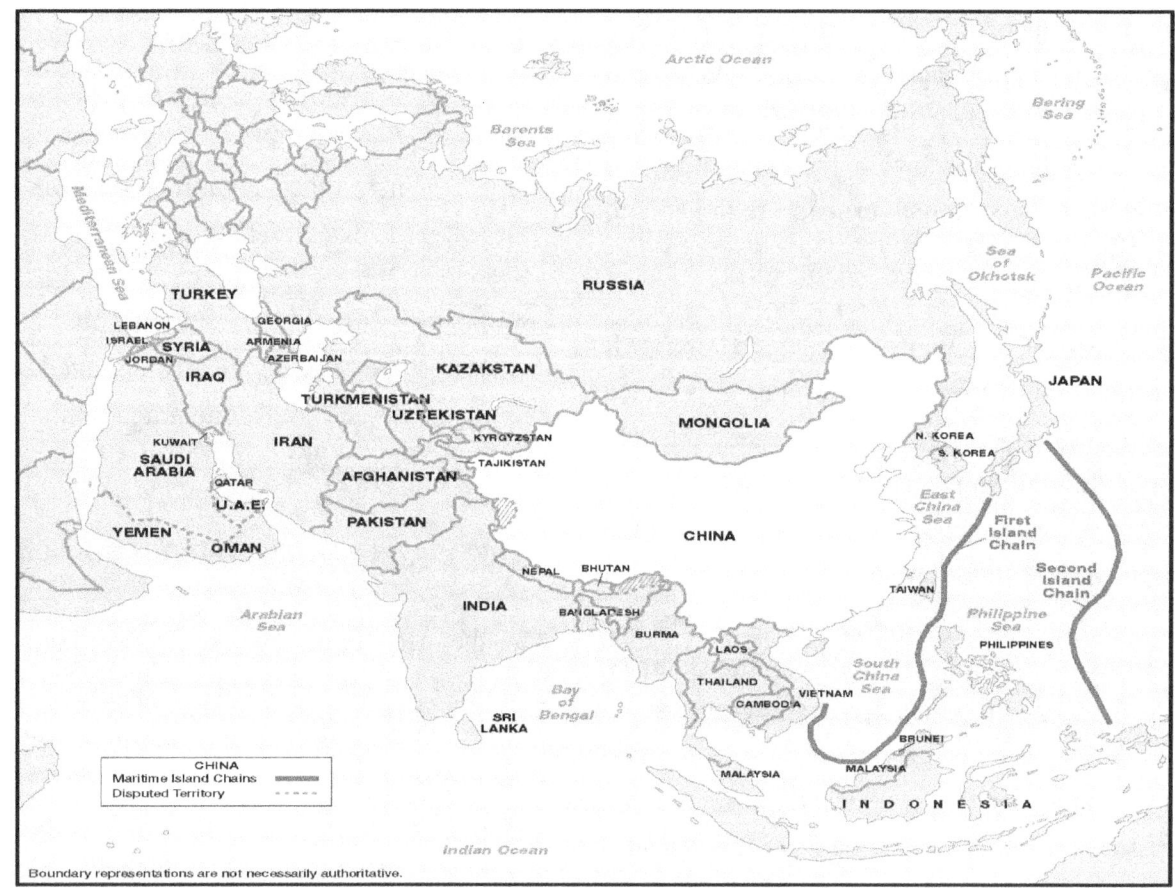

Figure 2. The First and Second Island Chains. *PRC military theorists conceive of two island "chains" as forming a geographic basis for China's maritime defensive perimeter.*

preemptive and coercive options it would provide China in a regional crisis.

Chinese military analysts have also concluded that logistics and mobilization are potential vulnerabilities in modern warfare, given the heavy requirements for precisely coordinated transportation, communications, and logistics networks. To threaten in-theater bases and logistics points, China could employ its theater ballistic missiles, land-attack cruise missiles, special operations forces, and computer network attacks. Strike aircraft, enabled by aerial refueling, could engage distant targets using air-launched cruise missiles equipped with a variety of terminal-homing warheads.

Advanced mines, submarines, maritime strike aircraft, and modern surface combatants equipped with advanced ASCMs would provide a supporting layer of defense for its long-range anti-access systems. Acquisition of the KILO, SONG,

---

Building Capacity for Conventional Precision Strike

Short-Range Ballistic Missiles (SRBMs) (< 1000 km). According to DIA estimates, as of October 2006 the PLA had roughly 900 SRBMs and is increasing its inventory at a rate of more than 100 missiles per year. The PLA's first-generation SRBMs do not possess true "precision strike" capability, but later generations have greater ranges and improved accuracy.

Medium-Range Ballistic Missiles (MRBMs) (1000-3000 km). The PLA is acquiring conventional MRBMs, apparently to increase the range to which it can conduct precision strikes, to include their possible use in targeting naval ships operating far from China's shores.

Land-Attack Cruise Missiles (LACMs). China is developing LACMs for stand-off, precision strike capability against hard-targets. First- and second-generation LACMs may be deployed in the near future.

Air-to-Surface Missiles (ASMs). China is believed to have a small number of tactical ASMs and precision-guided munitions, including all-weather, satellite-guided and laser-guided bombs, and is pursuing foreign and domestic acquisitions to improve airborne anti-ship capabilities.

Anti-Ship Cruise Missiles (ASCMs). PLA Navy has or is acquiring nearly a dozen varieties of ASCMs, from the 1950s-era CSS-N-2/STYX to the modern Russian-made SS-N-22/SUNBURN and SS-N-27B/SIZZLER. The pace of indigenous ASCM research, development and production – and of foreign procurement – has accelerated over the past decade.

Anti-Radiation Weapons. The PLA has imported Israeli-made HARPY UCAVs and Russian-made anti-radiation missiles, and is developing an anti-radiation missile based on the Russian Kh-31P (AS-17) known domestically as the YJ-91.

Artillery-Delivered High Precision Munitions. The PLA is deploying the A-100 300 mm multiple rocket launcher (MRL) (100+ km range) and developing the WS-2 400 mm MRL (200 km range). Additional munitions are being fielded or are under development.

SHANG, and YUAN-class submarines illustrates the importance the PLA places on undersea warfare. The purchase of SOVREMENNYY II-class DDGs and indigenous production of the LUYANG I/ LUYANG II DDGs equipped with long-range ASCM and SAM systems demonstrate a continuing emphasis on improving anti-surface warfare, combined with mobile, wide-area air control.

PLA air defense has shifted from point defense of key military, industrial, and political targets to a new Joint Anti-Air Raid Campaign based on a modern, integrated air defense system and offensive and defensive counter-air operations. These operations extend beyond the defense of Chinese airspace to include strikes against an adversary's bases (including aircraft carriers) and logistics to degrade the adversary's ability to conduct air operations.

The air defense component of anti-access/area-denial includes SAMs such as the SA-10, SA-20, HQ-9, HQ-15, and extended-range C2 suites such as the S-300PMU2. Beijing will also use Russian-built and domestic fourth-generation aircraft (e.g., Su-27 and Su-30 FLANKER variants, and the indigenous F-10). The PLA Navy would employ recently acquired Russian Su-30MK2 fighters, armed with AS-17/Kh-31A anti-ship missiles. The acquisition of refueling aircraft, including the Russian IL-78/MIDAS and the indigenously developed B-6U refueling aircraft, will extend operational ranges for PLAAF and PLA Navy strike aircraft armed with precision munitions, thereby increasing the threat to surface and air forces distant from China's coast. Additionally, acquisition of UAVs and UCAVs, including the Israeli HARPY, expands China's options for long-range reconnaissance and strike.

A final element of an emerging area denial/anti access strategy includes the electromagnetic, or information, sphere. PLA authors often cite the need in modern warfare to control information, sometimes termed an "information blockade." China is pursuing this ability by improving information and operational security, developing electronic warfare and information warfare capabilities, and denial and deception. China's concept of an "information blockade" likely extends beyond the strictly military realm to include other elements of state power. Secrecy, information controls (including internet security), and propaganda remain hallmarks of CCP rule.

In 2006, several independent researchers used a U.S.-based commercial imagery service provider's archive of overhead imagery to identify several Chinese military-related facilities including a submarine base, a facility that appeared to replicate a contested portion of the Sino-Indian border, and a mock Taiwan airfield. Shortly after the publication of these studies, Chinese state-run media in August 2006 claimed that foreign map makers had illegally surveyed Chinese territory and threatened China's security. The article referenced China's 2002 Surveying and Mapping Law and quoted the PRC State Bureau of Survey and Mapping as stating that "foreigners who illegally survey, gather and publish geographical information on China will be severely punished." This sequence of events may indicate that China is attempting to lay the groundwork to extend the concept of the "information blockade" into space.

Strategic Capabilities

Nuclear Deterrence. China is qualitatively and quantitatively improving its legacy strategic forces. These presently consist of approximately 20 silo-based, liquid-fueled CSS-4 ICBMs (which constitute its primary nuclear means of holding continental U.S. targets at risk), approximately 20 liquid-fueled, limited range CSS-3 ICBMs, between 14-18 liquid-fueled CSS-2 intermediate range ballistic missiles (IRBMs) and upwards of

50 CSS-5 road mobile, solid-fueled medium range ballistic missiles (MRBMs) (for regional deterrence missions), and JL-1 SLBMs on the XIA-class SSBN.

By 2010, China's strategic nuclear forces will likely comprise a combination of enhanced CSS-4s; CSS-3s; CSS-5s; solid-fueled, road-mobile DF-31s (which achieved initial threat availability in 2006, and will likely achieve operational status in the near future, if it has not already done so), and DF-31A ICBMs (expected IOC in 2007); and the JL-1 and JL-2 SLBMs (expected IOC between 2007-10). The addition of the DF-31 family of missiles and the JL-2 and JIN-class SSBNs will give China a more survivable and flexible nuclear force. New air- and ground-launched cruise missiles that could perform nuclear missions will similarly improve the survivability and flexibility of China's nuclear forces.

China's 2006 Defense White Paper states that: 1) the purpose China's nuclear force is to "deter other countries from using or threatening to use nuclear weapons against China;" 2) China "upholds the principles of counterattack in self-defense and limited development of nuclear weapons;" and, 3) China "has never entered into and will never enter into a nuclear arms race with any other country." The paper reiterated China's commitment to a declaratory policy of "no first use of nuclear weapons at any time and under any circumstances," and states China "unconditionally undertakes not to use or threaten to use nuclear weapons against non-nuclear-weapon states or nuclear weapon-free zones." Doctrinal materials suggest

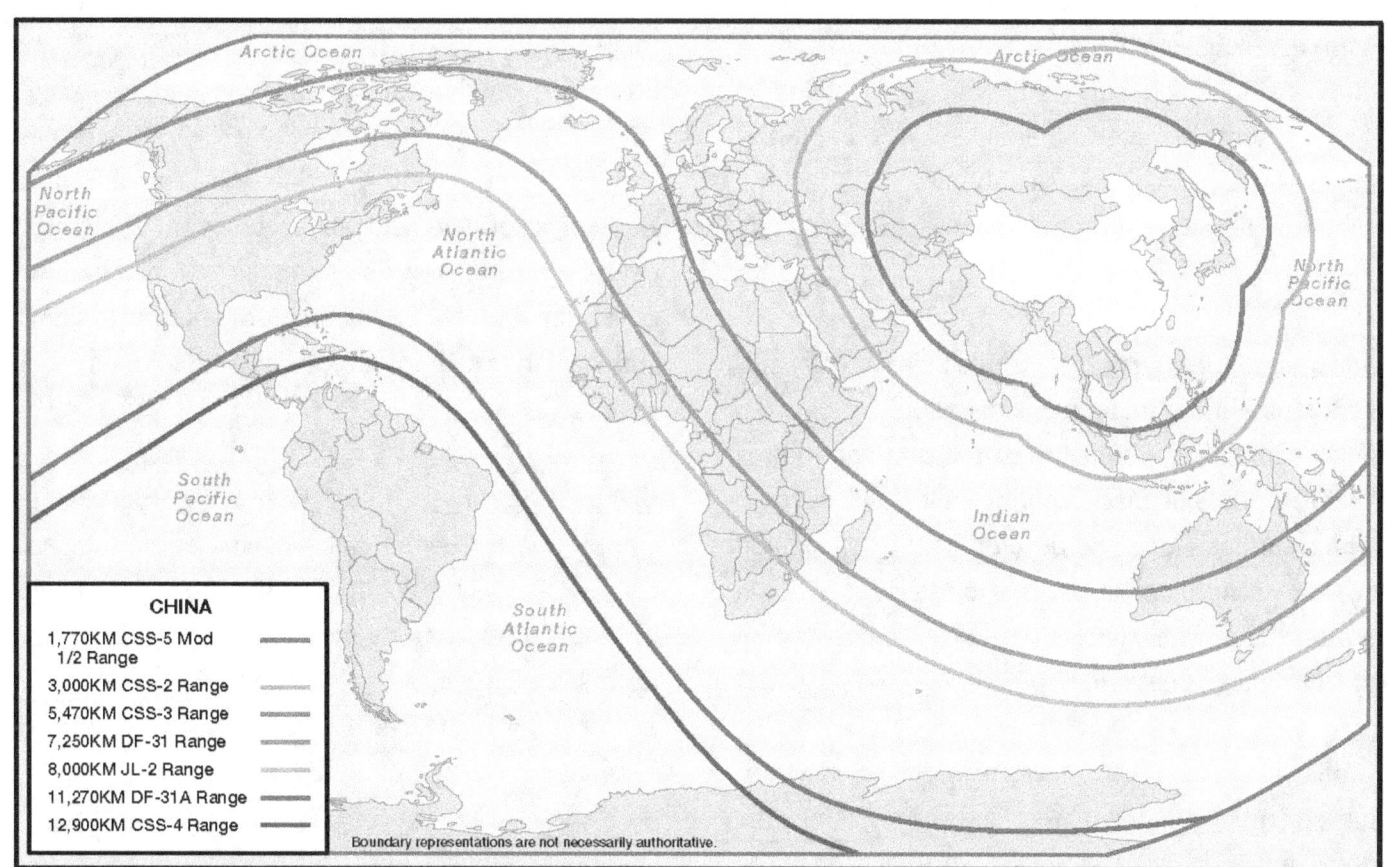

Figure 3. Medium and Intercontinental Range Ballistic Missiles. *China currently is capable of targeting its nuclear forces throughout the region and most of the world, including the continental United States. Newer systems, such as the DF-31, DF-31A, and JL-2, will give China a more survivable nuclear force.*

additional missions for China's nuclear forces include deterrence of conventional attacks against the Chinese mainland, reinforcing China's great power status, and increasing its freedom of action by limiting the extent to which others can coerce China. China's assertion of a nuclear "no first use" policy, therefore, is ambiguous. This ambiguity is compounded with the juxtaposition of the "no first use" declaration and the stated commitment to adhere to the principle of "counter attack in self defense."

Periodic military and civilian academic debates over the future of China's nuclear doctrine have questioned whether or not a "no first use" policy supports or detracts from China's deterrent, and whether or not "no first use" should remain in place. The Chinese government has provided public and private assurances that its "no first use" policy has not and will not change. Nevertheless, coupled with the debates themselves, the introduction of more capable and survivable nuclear systems in greater numbers suggest Beijing may be exploring the implications of China's evolving force structure, and the new options that force structure may provide.

Space and Counterspace. China's space activities and capabilities, including anti-satellite programs, have significant implications for anti-access/area denial in Taiwan Strait contingencies and beyond. China further views the development of space and counter-space capabilities as bolstering national prestige and, like nuclear weapons, demonstrating the attributes of a world power.

China has accorded space a high priority for investment. Premier Wen Jiabao, marking the 50th anniversary of China's aerospace industry in October 2006, stated that "China's aerospace industry is standing at a new starting point and facing a new situation and tasks." It is now

necessary, he said, "to implement the principle of independent innovations, leaps in key areas . . . carry out major state science and technology special projects in manned space flights and a lunar probe, and achieve new breakthroughs in research and development [of] aerospace equipment and . . . space technology."

Reconnaissance. China is deploying advanced imagery, reconnaissance, and Earth resource systems with military applications. Examples include the CBERS-1 and -2 satellites and the Huanjing disaster/environmental monitoring satellite constellation. China is planning eleven satellites in the Huanjing program capable of visible, infrared, multi-spectral, and synthetic aperture radar imaging. In the next decade, Beijing most likely will field radar, ocean surveillance, and high-resolution photoreconnaissance satellites. In the interim, China probably will rely on commercial satellite imagery (e.g., SPOT, LANDSAT, RADARSAT, and Ikonos) to supplement existing coverage.

Navigation and Timing. China has launched four BeiDou satellites with an accuracy of 20 meters over China and surrounding areas. China also uses GPS and GLONASS navigation satellite systems, and has invested in the EU's Galileo navigation system.

Manned Program. In October 2005, China completed its second manned space mission and Chinese astronauts conducted their first experiments in space. Press reports indicate China will perform its first space walk in 2007-2008, and rendezvous and docking in 2009-2012. China's goal is to have a manned space station by 2020.

Communications. China uses foreign providers, like INTELSAT and INMARSAT, for communications, but is expanding indigenous capabilities in this area. China may be developing a system of data relay satellites to support global coverage, and has reportedly acquired mobile data reception equipment that could support more rapid data transmission to deployed military forces and units.

Small Satellites. Since 2000, China has launched a number of small satellites, including an oceanographic research, imagery, and environmental research satellites. China has also established dedicated small satellite design and production facilities. China is developing microsatellites – weighing less than 100 kilograms – for remote sensing, and networks of imagery and radar satellites. These developments could allow for a rapid reconstitution or expansion of China's satellite force in the event of any disruption in coverage.

Anti-Satellite (ASAT) Weapons. In January 2007, China successfully tested a direct-ascent ASAT missile against a Chinese weather satellite, demonstrating its ability to attack satellites operating in low-Earth orbit. The direct ascent ASAT system is one component of a multi-dimensional program to generate the capability to deny others access to outer space.

In a PLA National Defense University book, Joint Space War Campaigns (2005), author Colonel Yuan Zelu writes:

> [The] goal of a space shock and awe strike is [to] deter the enemy, not to provoke the enemy into combat. For this reason, the objectives selected for strike must be few and precise . . .[for example] on important information sources, command and control centers, communications hubs, and other objectives. This will shake the structure of the opponent's operational system of organization and will create huge psychological impact on the opponent's policymakers.

China's nuclear arsenal has long provided Beijing with an inherent ASAT capability. However, in recent years Beijing has pursued a robust, multidimensional counterspace program. UHF-band satellite communications jammers acquired from Ukraine in the late 1990s and probable indigenous systems give China today the capacity to jam common satellite communications bands and GPS receivers. In addition to the direct ascent ASAT program demonstrated in January 2007, China is also developing other technologies and concepts for kinetic (hit-to-kill) weapons and directed-energy (e.g., lasers and radio frequency) weapons for ASAT missions. Citing the requirements of its manned and lunar space programs, China is improving its ability to track and identify satellites – a prerequisite for effective, precise physical attacks.

Information Warfare. There has been much writing on information warfare among China's military thinkers, who indicate a strong conceptual understanding of its methods and uses. For example, a November 2006 Liberation Army Daily commentator argued:

> [The] mechanism to get the upper hand of the enemy in a war under conditions of informatization finds prominent expression in whether or not we are capable of using various means to obtain information and of ensuring the effective circulation of information; whether or not we are capable of making full use of the permeability, sharable property, and connection of information to realize the organic merging of materials, energy, and information to form a combined fighting strength; [and,] whether or not we are capable of applying effective means to weaken the enemy side's information superiority and lower the operational efficiency of enemy information equipment.

The PLA is investing in electronic countermeasures, defenses against electronic attack (e.g., electronic and infrared decoys, angle reflectors, and false target generators), and computer network operations (CNO). China's CNO concepts include computer network attack, computer network defense, and computer network exploitation. The PLA sees CNO as critical to achieving "electromagnetic dominance" early in a conflict. Although there is no evidence of a formal Chinese CNO doctrine, PLA theorists have coined the term "Integrated Network Electronic Warfare" to prescribe the use of electronic warfare, CNO, and kinetic strikes to disrupt battlefield network information systems.

The PLA has established information warfare units to develop viruses to attack enemy computer systems and networks, and tactics and measures to protect friendly computer systems and networks. In 2005, the PLA began to incorporate offensive CNO into its exercises, primarily in first strikes against enemy networks.

Power Projection – Modernization Beyond Taiwan

In a speech at the March 2006 National People's Congress, PLA Chief of the General Staff Liang Guanglie stated that "one must attend to the effective implementation of the historical mission of our forces at this new stage in this new century. . . . preparations for a multitude of military hostilities must be done in concrete manner, [and] . . . competence in tackling multiple security threats and accomplishing a diverse range of military missions must be stepped up."

Consistent with this guidance, China continues to invest in military programs designed to improve extended-range power projection. Current trends in China's military capabilities are a major factor in changing East Asian military balances, and could provide China with a force capable of prosecuting a range of military operations in Asia – well beyond Taiwan. Given the apparent absence of direct threats from other nations, the purposes to which China's current and future military power will be applied remain unknown. It is certain, however, that these capabilities will increase Beijing's options for military coercion to press diplomatic advantage, advance interests, or resolve disputes.

The principal focus of, and driver for, China's military modernization in the near term appears to remain preparing for potential conflict in the Taiwan Strait. However, official documents and the writings of Chinese military strategists suggest Beijing is increasingly surveying the strategic landscape beyond Taiwan. Some Chinese analysts have explored the geopolitical value of Taiwan in extending China's maritime "defensive" perimeter and improving its ability to influence regional sea lines of communication. For example, the PLA Academy of Military Science text, *Science of Military Strategy* (2000), states:

> *If Taiwan should be alienated from the mainland, not only [would] our natural maritime defense system lose its depth, opening a sea gateway to outside forces, but also a large area of water territory and rich resources of ocean resources would fall into the hands of others. . . . [O]ur line of foreign trade and transportation which is vital to China's opening up and economic development will be exposed to the surveillance and threats of separatists and enemy forces, and China will forever be locked to the west of the first chain of islands in the West Pacific.*

China's 2006 Defense White Paper similarly raises concerns about resources and transportation links when it states that "security issues related to energy, resources, finance, information, and international shipping routes are mounting." The related desire to protect energy investments in Central Asia and could also provide an incentive for military investment or intervention if instability surfaces in the region. Disagreements that remain with Japan over maritime claims and with several Southeast Asian claimants to all or parts of the Spratly Islands in the South China Sea could lead to renewed tensions in these areas. Instability on the Korean Peninsula likewise could produce a regional crisis in which Beijing would face a choice between a diplomatic or a military response.

Analysis of China's weapons acquisitions also suggests China is looking beyond Taiwan as it builds its force. For example, new missile units outfitted with conventional theater-range missiles at various locations in China could be used in a variety of non-Taiwan contingencies. Airborne early warning and control and aerial-refueling programs will permit extended air operations into the South China Sea. Advanced destroyers and submarines reflect Beijing's desire to protect and advance its maritime interests. Expeditionary forces (three airborne divisions, two amphibious infantry divisions, two marine brigades, about seven special operations groups, and one regimental-size reconnaissance element in the Second Artillery) are improving with the introduction of new equipment, better unit-level tactics, and greater coordination of joint operations. Over the long term, improvements in China's C4ISR, including space-based and over-the-horizon sensors, could enable Beijing to identify, track and target military activities deep into the western Pacific Ocean.

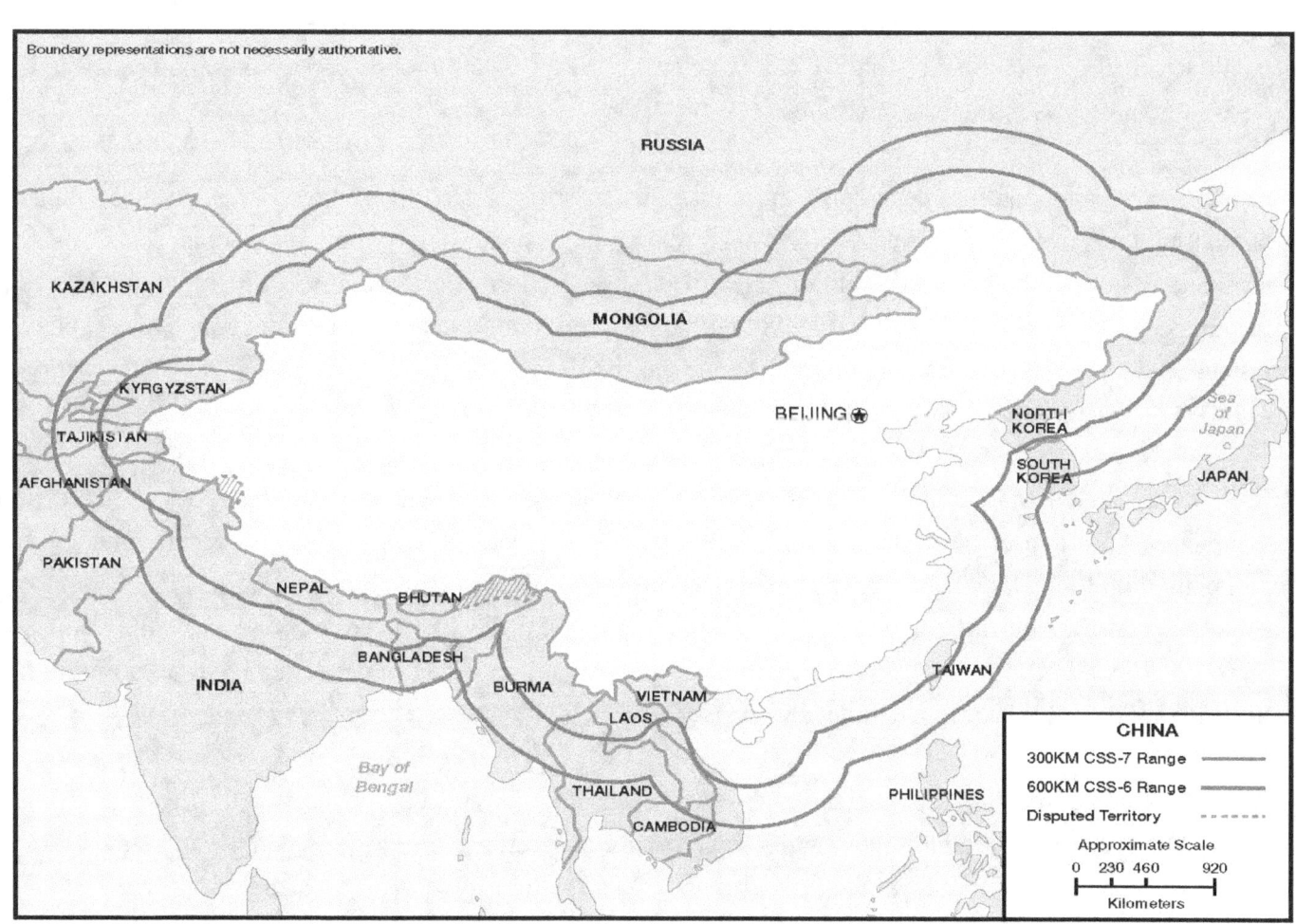

Figure 4. Maximum Ranges for China's Conventional SRBM Force. *China currently is capable of deploying ballistic missile forces to support a variety of regional contingencies.*

Finally, analysis of PLA training activities provides an additional indication that the PLA is exploring contingencies other than Taiwan. For example, the July-August 2006 North Sword-07, a simulated, opposing-forces exercise, involved for the first time two fully equipped PLA divisions with the support of the air force, Second Artillery Corps, and the People's Armed Police. The exercise focused on long-distance maneuver, intelligence acquisition, and mobile counterattack operations.

China in 2006 also conducted a series of exercises with the Shanghai Cooperation Organization (SCO) with the stated objective of fighting the "three evil forces" of international terrorism, religious extremism, and national separatism, including:

- "Tianshan-1 2006," a bilateral exercise with Kazakhstan in August 2006, which took place in Almaty, Kazakhstan and Yining, China improved cooperation between law enforcement and security departments.

- "Cooperation 2006," a bilateral exercise with Tajikistan in September 2006, featured 150 troops from China and 300 troops from Tajikistan in a scenario for coordinated responses to terrorist attacks.

Status of Aircraft Carrier Developments

In October 2006, Lieutenant General Wang Zhiyuan, vice chairman of the Science and Technology Commission of the PLA's General Armament Department stated that the "Chinese army will study how to manufacture aircraft carriers so that we can develop our own . . . . [A]ircraft carriers are indispensable if we want to protect our interests in oceans."

China first began to discuss developing an indigenous aircraft carrier in the late 1970s. In 1985, China purchased the Australian carrier the HMAS Melbourne. Although the hull was scrapped, Chinese technicians studied the ship and built a replica of its flight deck for pilot training. China purchased two former Soviet carriers – the Minsk in 1998 and the Kiev in 2000. Neither carrier was made operational; instead, they were used as floating military theme parks. Nevertheless, both provided design information to PLA Navy engineers.

In 1998 China purchased the ex-Varyag, a Kuznetsov-class Soviet carrier that was only 70 percent complete at the time of the Soviet Union's collapse. Recent deck refurbishment, electrical work, fresh hull paint with PLA Navy markings, and expressed interest in Russia's Su-33 fighter has re-kindled debate about a Chinese carrier fleet. The PLA's ultimate intentions for the Varyag remain unclear, but a number of possibilities exist: turning it into an operational aircraft carrier, a training or transitional platform, or a floating theme park – its originally-stated purpose.

Regardless of Beijing's final objective for the ex-Varyag, PLA Navy study of the ship's structural design could eventually assist China in creating its own carrier program. Lieutenant General Wang stated that, "we cannot establish a real naval force of aircraft carriers within three or five years." Some analysts in and out of government predict that China could have an operational carrier by the end of the 12th Five-Year Plan (2011-2015); others assess the earliest it could deploy an operational aircraft carrier is 2020 or beyond.

Chapter Five
Resources for Force Modernization

" . . . uphold the scientific development concept as the important guiding principle in strengthening national defense and army building; push national defense and army building forward in a faster and better way . . ."

– Hu Jintao

Overview

Sources for PLA modernization include domestic defense expenditures, indigenous defense industrial developments, and foreign technology acquisition – all of which are driven by the performance of the economy. China's economic growth has enabled Beijing to invest ever increasing resources in its defense sector over the past 15 years.

As its domestic defense industry matures, China is acquiring foreign weapons and technology, primarily from Russia, to fill near-term capability gaps. In the long term, however, Beijing seeks a wholly indigenous defense industrial sector. China's defense industries benefit from foreign direct investment and joint ventures in the civilian sector, technical knowledge and expertise of students returned from abroad, and state-sponsored industrial espionage. The EU arms embargo not only remains an important symbolic and moral restraint on EU countries' military interactions with the PLA, but a lifting of the embargo would expand China's access to military and dual-use technology to improve current weapon systems and develop indigenous capabilities to produce future systems.

Military Expenditure Trends

On March 4, 2007, Beijing announced a 17.8 percent increase in its military budget, bringing its official defense budget figure for 2007 to approximately $45 billion. This development continues a trend of annual budget increases that exceed significantly growth of the overall economy.

Analysis of PRC budget data and International Monetary Fund (IMF) GDP data for the period of 1996 to 2006 shows average annual defense budget growth of 11.8 percent (inflation adjusted) compared with average annual GDP growth of 9.2 percent (inflation adjusted). Of note, China's 2006 Defense White Paper contains a similar analysis in stating that between 1990 and 2005 the defense budget grew by an average of 9.6 percent between, while China's GDP over the same period grew in constant prices an average of 9.7 percent yearly, according to the IMF. The 1996-2006 data is a more useful measure, however, as it covers the period following the 1995 and 1996 Taiwan Strait crises and incorporates the 9th and 10th Five Year Plan periods (1996-2000 and 2001-2005, respectively) in which the post-Persian Gulf War re-invigoration of the PLA modernization drive would be fully reflected.

Substantial growth in China's defense budget aside, China's published defense budget does not include large categories of expenditure, including expenses for strategic forces, foreign acquisitions, military-related research and development, and China's paramilitary forces. The Defense Intelligence Agency (DIA) estimates China's total military-related spending for 2007 could be as much as $85 billion to $125 billion.

Accurately estimating Chinese military expenditures is a difficult process due to the lack of accounting transparency and China's failure to comply with international standards for reporting military expenditures and funding. As a result, outside estimates of China's military spending vary widely. For example, select government and independent calculations for the PLA's expenditures for 2003 – the most recent year for which a significant number of institutions published estimates – ranged from $30.6 billion to $141 billion based on official exchange rates or purchasing power parity (PPP) models. China's declared budget in that year, in contrast, was $22.3 billion.

The United States and other countries have, for many years, urged China to increase transparency in defense spending. To date, Beijing has provided only highly aggregated military budget data in its Defense White Papers. Moreover, some Chinese officials remain opposed to candid dialogue on the subject. In response to an August 2006 press question on transparency in PLA budgeting, the PRC's UN Ambassador in Geneva, Sha Zukang, asserted bluntly that "it's better for the U.S. to shut up and keep quiet" about it.

China's Advancing Defense Industries

Defense industry modernization accelerated in the mid-1990s based on reforms to rationalize military procurement and increase innovation among China's state-owned defense companies. These reforms have enabled the development and production of

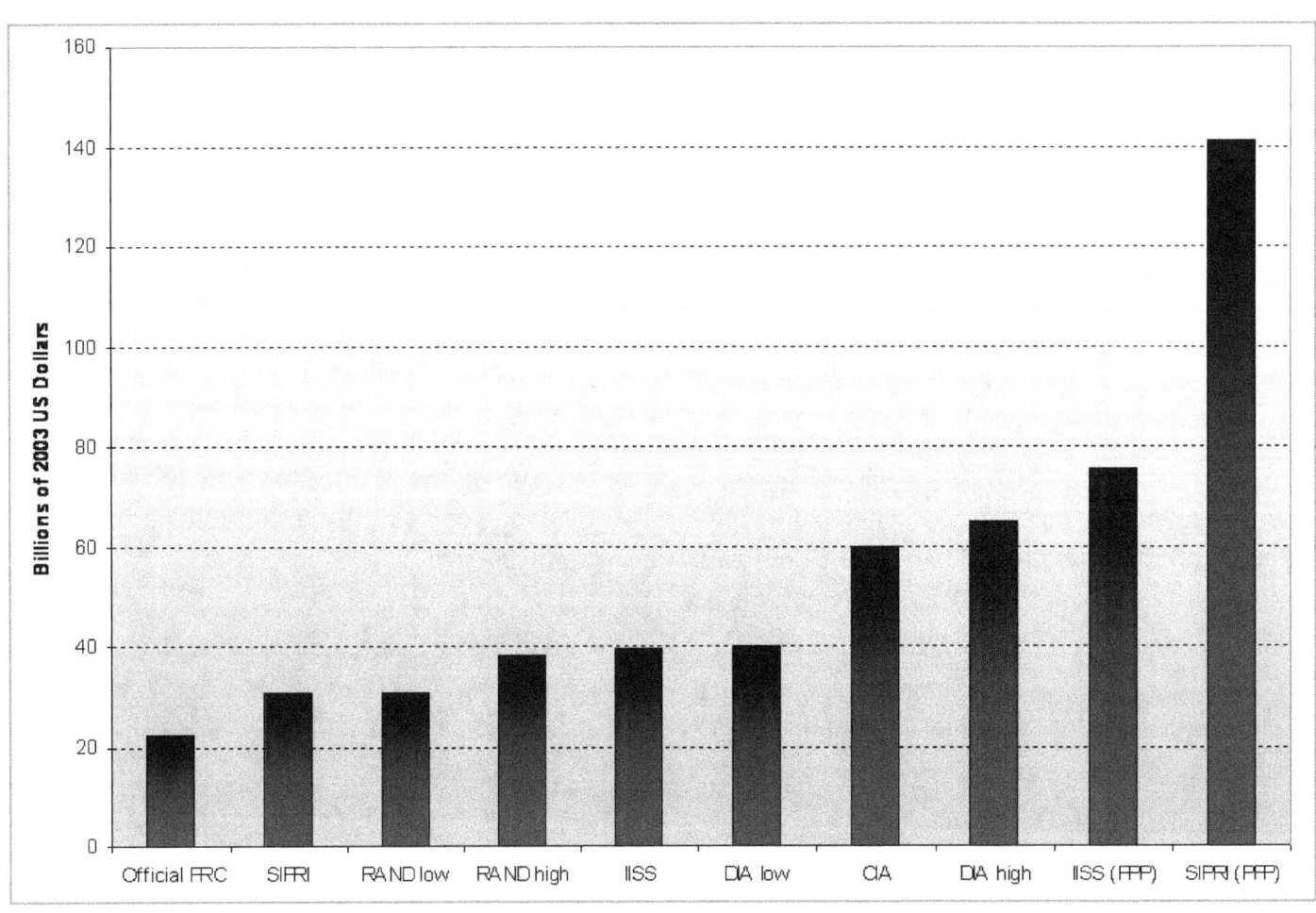

Figure 5. Comparison of Outside Estimates of PRC Military Spending. *Government and research institutes have developed various – but often incompatible – methods to account for the PLA's off-budget expenditures and sources of income, and other factors. Two different exchange rate models – official exchange rate and purchasing power parity indices – further complicate estimates of China's defense spending. Estimates above are in 2003 U.S. dollars based on official exchange rates unless otherwise indicated.*

Military Power of the People's Republic of China

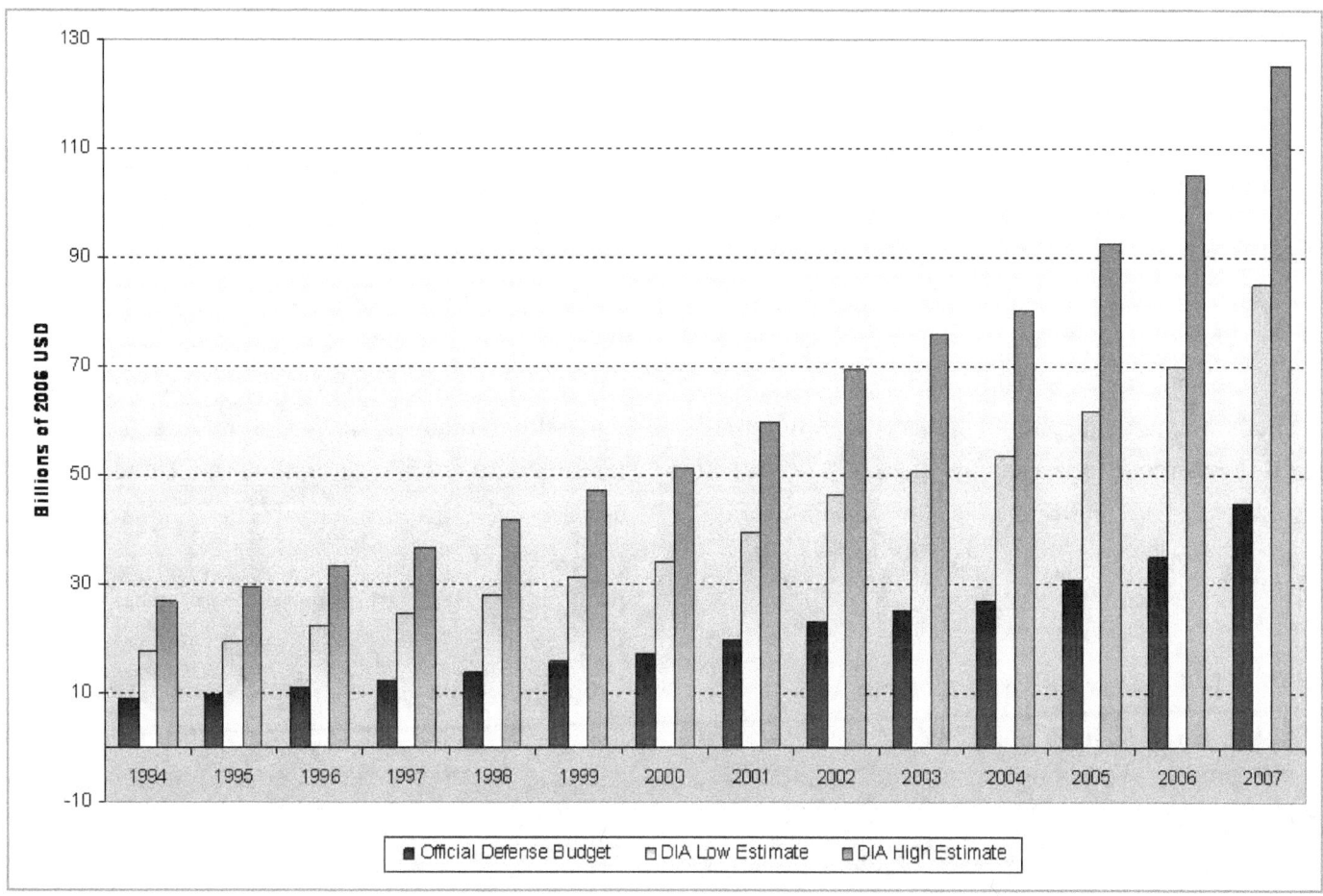

Figure 6. Chinese Defense Budget and Estimates of Total Defense-Related Expenditures. *The graphic depicts China official defense budget since 1994, and associated Defense Intelligence Agency estimates of actual defense expenditure. All figures in 2006 US Dollars.*

select weapon systems, such as missiles, fighter jets, and warships, approaching performance parameters comparable to Western systems.

Missile and Space Industry. China develops and produces a broad range of ballistic, cruise, and surface-to-air missiles. Improved production capabilities will enable China to more efficiently address force modernization goals by enhancing production of existing missile designs and supporting the development of new cruise and ballistic missiles with longer ranges and precision strike capabilities. China's space launch vehicle industry is expanding to support the national emphasis on satellite launch capability and the manned space program. China hopes to have more than 100 satellites in orbit by 2010, and to launch

an additional 100 satellites by 2020.

Shipbuilding Sector. In the last five years, China's shipyard expansions, mainly in the commercial container ship market, have increased China's overall shipbuilding capacity. Dual-purpose (military/civilian) shipyards are capable of supporting construction of major combatants, large amphibious ships, and supertankers. China is capable of serial production of modern diesel-electric submarines and is moving forward with new nuclear submarines. China continues to rely on foreign suppliers for propulsion units, and to a lesser degree for weapons systems, sensors, and other advanced electronics- and materials-based ship-borne technologies.

Aircraft Production. China's commercial and military aviation industry has advanced from producing direct copies of early Soviet models to developing and producing indigenous aircraft. China is producing improved versions of older aircraft as well as modern fourth generation fighters, and is developing a fifth generation combat aircraft. China continues to seek Russian and other foreign assistance in areas such as engines and avionics. China's commercial aircraft industry has imported high-precision and technologically advanced machine tools, electronics, and other components. This dual-use technology can also be used in the production of military aircraft.

Beijing is decreasing reliance on foreign assistance, improving business practices, streamlining bureaucracy, shortening development timelines, boosting quality control, and increasing production capacity for military orders. As part of these efforts, China's 11th Five-Year Plan aims to strengthen the defense-related scientific, technical, and industrial bases. These defense-related industries will continue to reap benefits from:

- Transfers of technology and skills from foreign joint ventures.

- Increased government funding for research, development, and procurement.

- Legal and illegal acquisition of foreign military and dual-use technology.

- Increased partnerships with academic institutions, which improve student recruitment and technical training for existing staff.

- China's reverse brain drain. Many of China's new generation of scientists, engineers, and managers are returning to China after receiving training and gaining experience abroad.

Foreign Weapons and Technology Acquisition

In 2005, China signed arms agreements with foreign suppliers worth almost $2.8 billion, making it the third largest arms recipient among developing countries. Russia remains China's primary weapons and materiel provider, selling it advanced fighter aircraft, missile systems, submarines, and destroyers. China is currently negotiating the purchase of additional surface-to-air missiles, combat aircraft, aircraft engines, and assault and transport helicopters. China relies on Russian components for several of its production programs and has purchased production rights to Russian weapon designs. Russia cooperates with China on technical, design, and material support for numerous weapons and space systems; for example China's *Shenzhou* manned space module is based on the Russian *Soyuz* capsule.

Israel has also historically been a supplier of advanced military technology to China. The Israelis transferred HARPY UCAVs to China in 2001 and conducted maintenance on HARPY parts during 2003-2004. In 2005, Israel began to improve government oversight of exports to China by strengthening controls of military exports, establishing controls on dual-use exports, and increasing the role of the Ministry of Foreign Affairs in export-related decisions. In January 2007, Israel implemented new dual-use export controls, based on the Wassenaar Arrangement. As of February 2007, legislation pending in the Knesset would adopt Wassenaar controls on munitions list exports. It remains unclear to what extent the new export controls will prevent additional sensitive military-related transfers to Beijing in the future.

Despite their history of strong arms trade relationships with China, Russia and Israel have usually refrained from transferring their most sophisticated weapons systems to China. To diversify its arms supplier base and acquire advanced technology, the PRC is looking to alternative suppliers such as Europe. Since 2003 China has been pressuring EU states to lift the embargo on lethal military sales to China that the EU imposed in response to the PRC's 1989 crackdown on Tiananmen Square demonstrators. In their Joint Statement following the 2004 EU-China Summit, European leaders committed to work towards lifting the embargo, a pledge they repeated in 2005 and 2006. Although the issue officially remains on the EU agenda, the current political sentiment among most Member States remains opposed to lifting the embargo in the near future.

Some Member States have advocated eliminating the embargo in the context of making the EU's enhanced "Code of Conduct" on arms exports binding; the Code governs arms transfers to third countries but is currently a voluntary instrument. Although some in the EU have argued that ending the embargo and instead subjecting exports to China to the terms of the Code of Conduct would result in no qualitative or quantitative increases in China's military capabilities, other EU members remain concerned, as does the United States, that the provisions of the Code remain inadequate.

Lifting the EU embargo would likely contribute significantly to the PLA's modernization goals. An end to the embargo would raise the possibility of competitive pricing for arms sales to China, giving Beijing leverage to pressure its existing suppliers – including Russia, Israel, and Ukraine – to provide even more advanced weapons and favorable terms of sale. Increased military-to-military exchanges consequent to arms sales resulting from lifting the embargo could also give the PLA access to critical military management practices, operational doctrine, and training. Finally, the transfer of sophisticated military and dual-use technologies that China most likely desires from the EU – C4ISR components and systems, advanced space technology, radar systems, early-warning aircraft, submarine technology, and advanced electronics for precision-guided weapons – would advance PLA operational capabilities.

China continues a systematic effort to obtain from abroad through legal and illegal commercial transactions dual-use and military technologies. Many dual-use technologies, such as software, integrated circuits, computers, electronics, semiconductors, telecommunications, and information security systems, are vital for the PLA's transformation into an information-based, network-centric force. Several high profile legal cases highlight China's efforts to obtain sensitive U.S. technologies (e.g., missile, imaging, semiconductor, and submarine) illegally by targeting well-placed scientists and businessmen. U.S. Immigration and Customs Enforcement (ICE) officials have rated China's aggressive and wide-ranging espionage as the leading threat to U.S. technology. Since 2000, ICE has initiated more than 400 investigations involving the illicit export of U.S. arms and technologies to China.

Chapter Six
Force Modernization and Security in the Taiwan Strait

"The struggle to oppose and contain the separatist forces for 'Taiwan independence' and their activities remains a hard one. By pursuing a radical policy for 'Taiwan independence,' the Taiwan authorities aim at creating 'de jure independence' through 'constitutional reform,' thus still posing a grave threat to China's sovereignty and territorial integrity. "

– China's National Defense in 2006

Overview

The security situation in the Taiwan Strait is largely a function of dynamic interactions among policies and actions taken by the mainland, Taiwan, and the United States. China's emergence as a global economic force, increased diplomatic clout, and improved air, naval, and missile forces strengthen Beijing's position relative to Taipei by increasing the mainland's economic leverage over Taiwan, fostering Taiwan's diplomatic isolation, and shifting the cross-Strait military balance in the mainland's favor. Taiwan, meanwhile, has allowed its defense spending to decline in real terms over the past decade, creating an increased urgency for the Taiwan authorities to make the necessary investments to maintain the island's self-defense capabilities. The U.S. Government has made clear that it opposes unilateral changes to the status quo by either side of the Taiwan Strait, does not support Taiwan independence, and supports peaceful resolution of cross-Strait differences in a manner acceptable to the people on both sides of the Taiwan Strait.

In accordance with the Taiwan Relations Act [Public Law 96-8, (1979)], the United States has taken steps to help maintain peace, security, and stability in the region. In addition to making available to Taiwan defense articles and services to enable Taiwan to maintain a sufficient self-defense capability, the U.S.

Department of Defense, through the transformation of U.S. Armed Forces and global force posture realignments, is maintaining the capacity to resist any effort by Beijing to resort to force or coercion to dictate the terms of Taiwan's future status. For its part, Taiwan has taken important steps to improve its joint operations capability, strengthen its officer and non-commissioned officer corps, build its reserve stocks, and improve crisis response capabilities. Taiwan has bolstered its defensive capabilities by taking delivery of the final two of four KIDD-class DDGs in September 2006. These improvements have, on the whole, reinforced Taiwan's natural defensive advantages in the face of Beijing's continuing build-up.

However, Taiwan has yet to acquire other major end items offered for sale by the United States in 2001, namely, Patriot PAC-3 air defense systems, P-3C Orion anti-submarine aircraft, and diesel electric submarines. These systems would enable Taiwan to make necessary improvements to its air and missile defense and anti-submarine warfare capability. In the six years since the offer was made, China has continued to make significant advances, some unexpected, in the capability areas these systems are designed to protect against.

China's Strategy in the Taiwan Strait

Beijing appears prepared to defer unification as long

as it believes trends are advancing toward that goal and that the costs of conflict outweigh the benefits. In the near term, Beijing's focus is likely one of preventing Taiwan from moving toward *de jure* independence while continuing to hold out terms for peaceful resolution under a "one country, two systems" framework that would provide Taiwan a degree of autonomy in exchange for its unification with the mainland. Beijing is pursuing these goals through a coercive strategy – with elements of persuasion – that integrates political, economic, cultural, legal, diplomatic, and military instruments of power.

Although Beijing professes peaceful resolution as its preferred outcome, the PLA's ongoing deployment of short range ballistic missiles, enhanced amphibious warfare capabilities, and modern, long-range anti-air systems opposite Taiwan are reminders of Beijing's refusal to renounce the use of force.

The sustained military threat to Taiwan serves as an important backdrop to the overall campaign of persuasion and coercion. Exercises, deployments, and media operations all contribute to an environment of intimidation. For example,

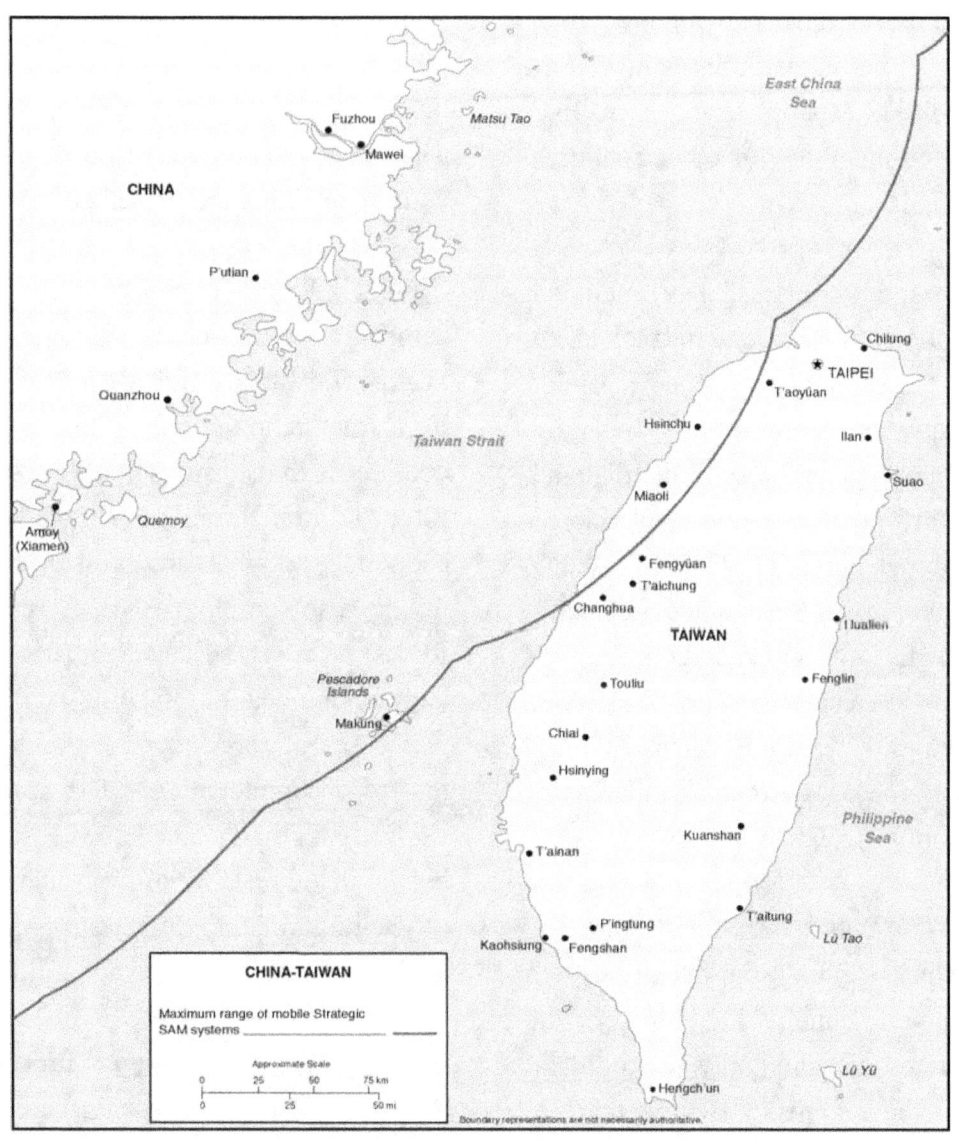

Figure 7. Taiwan Strait SAM coverage. *This map depicts notional coverage based on the range of the Russian-designed S-300PMU2 system equipped with the SA-20 SAM. Actual coverage would be non-contiguous and dependent upon precise deployment sites.*

in a March 2006 speech before military deputies to the National People's Congress plenary, China's Minister of National Defense, General Cao Gangchuan, noted that the Taiwan Strait situation was "still very grim and complicated," and proclaimed that, "all PLA officers and men must enhance their sense of imminent danger as well as their sense of mission and sense of responsibility, lose no time in making military preparations for military struggle, and resolutely safeguard national sovereignty and territorial integrity!"

The circumstances in which the mainland has historically warned it would use force against the island are not fixed and have evolved over time in response to Taiwan's declarations and actions relating to its political status, changes in PLA capabilities, and Beijing's view of other countries' relations with Taiwan.

These circumstances, or "red lines," have included: a formal declaration of Taiwan independence; undefined moves "toward independence"; foreign intervention in Taiwan's internal affairs; indefinite delays in the resumption of cross-Strait dialogue on unification; Taiwan's acquisition of nuclear weapons; and, internal unrest on Taiwan. Article 8 of the March 2005 "Anti-Secession Law" states Beijing would resort to "non-peaceful means" if "secessionist forces . . . cause the fact of Taiwan's secession from China," if "major incidents entailing Taiwan's secession" occur, or if "possibilities for peaceful reunification" are exhausted.

The ambiguity of these "red-lines" appears deliberate, allowing Beijing the flexibility to determine the nature, timing, and form of its response. Added to this ambiguity are political factors internal to the regime in Beijing that are opaque to outsiders.

Beijing's Courses of Action Against Taiwan

The PLA's capabilities to pursue a variety of courses of action are improving. In the absence of direct insights into PLA contingency planning, some analysts hold that Beijing would signal its readiness to use force imminently in an attempt to menace Taiwan in accordance with Beijing's dictates. Others assess that the likely Chinese course of action would be designed to create military and political pressure toward a rapid resolution on Beijing's terms before the United States or other countries would have a chance to respond. If a quick resolution is not possible, Beijing would seek to deter U.S. intervention or, failing that, delay such intervention, defeat it in an asymmetric, limited, quick war; or, fight it to a standstill and pursue a protracted conflict. Rough outlines for these courses of action are presented below.

Limited Force Options. A limited military campaign could include computer network attacks against Taiwan's political, military, and economic infrastructure to undermine the Taiwan population's confidence in its leadership. PLA special operations forces infiltrated into Taiwan could conduct acts of economic, political, and military sabotage. Beijing might also employ SRBM, special operations forces, and air strikes against air fields, radars, and communications facilities on Taiwan as "non-war" uses of force to push the Taiwan leadership toward accommodation. The apparent belief that significant kinetic attacks on Taiwan would pass below the threshold of war underscores the risk of Beijing making a catastrophic miscalculation leading to a major unintended military conflict.

Air and Missile Campaign. Surprise SRBM attacks and precision air strikes against Taiwan's air defense system, including air bases, radar sites, missiles, space assets, and communications facilities could support a campaign to degrade Taiwan defenses,

Factors of Deterrence

China is deterred on multiple levels from taking military action against Taiwan. First, China does not yet possess the military capability to accomplish with confidence its political objectives on the island, particularly when confronted with the prospect of U.S. intervention. Moreover, an insurgency directed against the PRC presence could tie up PLA forces for years. A military conflict in the Taiwan Strait would also affect the interests of Japan and other nations in the region in ensuring a peaceful resolution of the cross-Strait dispute.

Beijing's calculus would also have to factor in the potential political and economic repercussions of military conflict with Taiwan. China's leaders recognize that a war could severely retard economic development. Taiwan is China's single largest source of foreign direct investment, and an extended campaign would wreck Taiwan's economic infrastructure, leading to high reconstruction costs. International sanctions could further damage Beijing's economic development. A conflict would also severely damage the image that Beijing has sought to project in the post-Tiananmen years and would taint Beijing's hosting of the 2008 Olympics, for which China's leaders would almost certainly face boycotts and possibly a loss of the games. A conflict could also trigger domestic unrest on the mainland, a contingency that Beijing appears to have factored into its planning. Finally, China's leaders recognize that a conflict over Taiwan involving the United States would give rise to a long-term hostile relationship between the two nations – a result that would not be in China's interests.

neutralize its military and political leadership, and rapidly break its will to fight while attempting to preclude an effective international response.

Blockade. Beijing could threaten or deploy a naval blockade as a "non-war" pressure tactic in the pre-hostility phase or as a transition to active conflict. Beijing could declare that ships en route to Taiwan ports must stop in mainland ports for inspections prior to transiting on to Taiwan. It could also attempt the equivalent of a blockade by declaring exercise or missile closure areas in approaches and roadsteads to ports to divert merchant traffic, as occurred during the 1995-96 missile firings and live-fire exercises. Chinese doctrine also includes activities such as air blockades, missile attacks, and mining or otherwise obstructing harbors and approaches. More traditional blockades would have greater impact on Taiwan, but tax PLA Navy capabilities. Any attempt to limit maritime traffic to and from Taiwan would likely trigger countervailing international pressure, and risk military escalation. Such restrictions would have immediate economic effects, but would take time to realize decisive political results, diminishing the ultimate effectiveness and inviting international reaction.

Amphibious Invasion. Publicly available Chinese writings offer different strategies for an amphibious invasion of Taiwan, the most prominent being the Joint Island Landing Campaign. The Joint Island Landing Campaign envisions a complex operation relying on supporting sub-campaigns for logistics, electronic warfare, and air and naval support, to break through or circumvent shore defenses, establish and build a beachhead, and then launch an attack to split, seize, and occupy the entire island or key targets.

Amphibious operations are logistics-intensive, and their success depends upon air and sea superiority in the vicinity of the operation, the rapid build-up of supplies and sustainment on shore, and an uninterrupted flow of support thereafter. An amphibious campaign of the scale outlined in the Joint Island Landing Campaign would tax the capabilities of China's armed forces and almost certainly invite international intervention. Add to these strains the combat attrition of China's forces, and the complex tasks of urban warfare and counterinsurgency – assuming a successful landing and breakout – and an amphibious invasion of Taiwan would be a significant political and military risk for China's leaders.

(This page left intentionally blank)

APPENDIX
China and Taiwan Forces Data

Taiwan Strait Military Balance, Ground Forces			
China			**Taiwan**
	Total	**Taiwan Strait Area**	**Total**
Personnel (Active)	1.4 million	400,000	130,000
Group Armies	18	8	3
Infantry Divisions	25	9	0
Infantry Brigades	33	12	13
Armor Divisions/Brigades	9	4	0
Armor Brigades	11	4	5
Artillery Divisions	3	3	0
Artillery Brigades	15	5	3+
Marine Brigades	2	2	2
Tanks	7,000	2,700	1,800
Artillery Pieces	11,000	3,200	3,200

Note: The PLA active ground forces are organized into Group Armies. Infantry, armor, and artillery units are organized into a combination of divisions and brigades deployed throughout the PLA's seven Military Regions (MRs). A significant portion of these assets are deployed in the Taiwan Strait area, specifically the Nanjing, Guangzhou, and Jinan military regions. Figures for the Taiwan Strait area do not include the 15th Airborne Corps and garrison units. In 2004, Taiwan began transforming motorized rifle and armored infantry brigades to mechanized infantry. Taiwan has seven Defense Commands, three of which have Group Armies. Each Army contains an Artillery Command roughly equivalent to a brigade plus.

Figure 8. *Taiwan Strait Military Balance, Ground Forces*

Figure 9. *Major Ground Force Units*

Taiwan Strait Military Balance, Air Forces			
China			Taiwan
Aircraft	Total	Within range of Taiwan	Total
Fighters	1,550	425	330
Bombers	775	275	0
Transport	450	75	40

Note: The PLAAF and PLA Navy have a total of around 2,325 operational combat aircraft: air defense and multi-role fighters, ground attack aircraft, fighter-bombers, and bombers. An additional 470 older fighters and bombers are assigned to PLA flight academies or R&D. The two air arms also possess approximately 450 transports and over 90 surveillance and reconnaissance aircraft with photographic, surface search, and airborne early warning sensors. The majority of PLAAF and PLA Navy aircraft are based in the eastern part of the country. Currently, more than 700 aircraft could conduct combat operations against Taiwan without refueling.

Figure 10. *Taiwan Strait Military Balance, Air Forces*

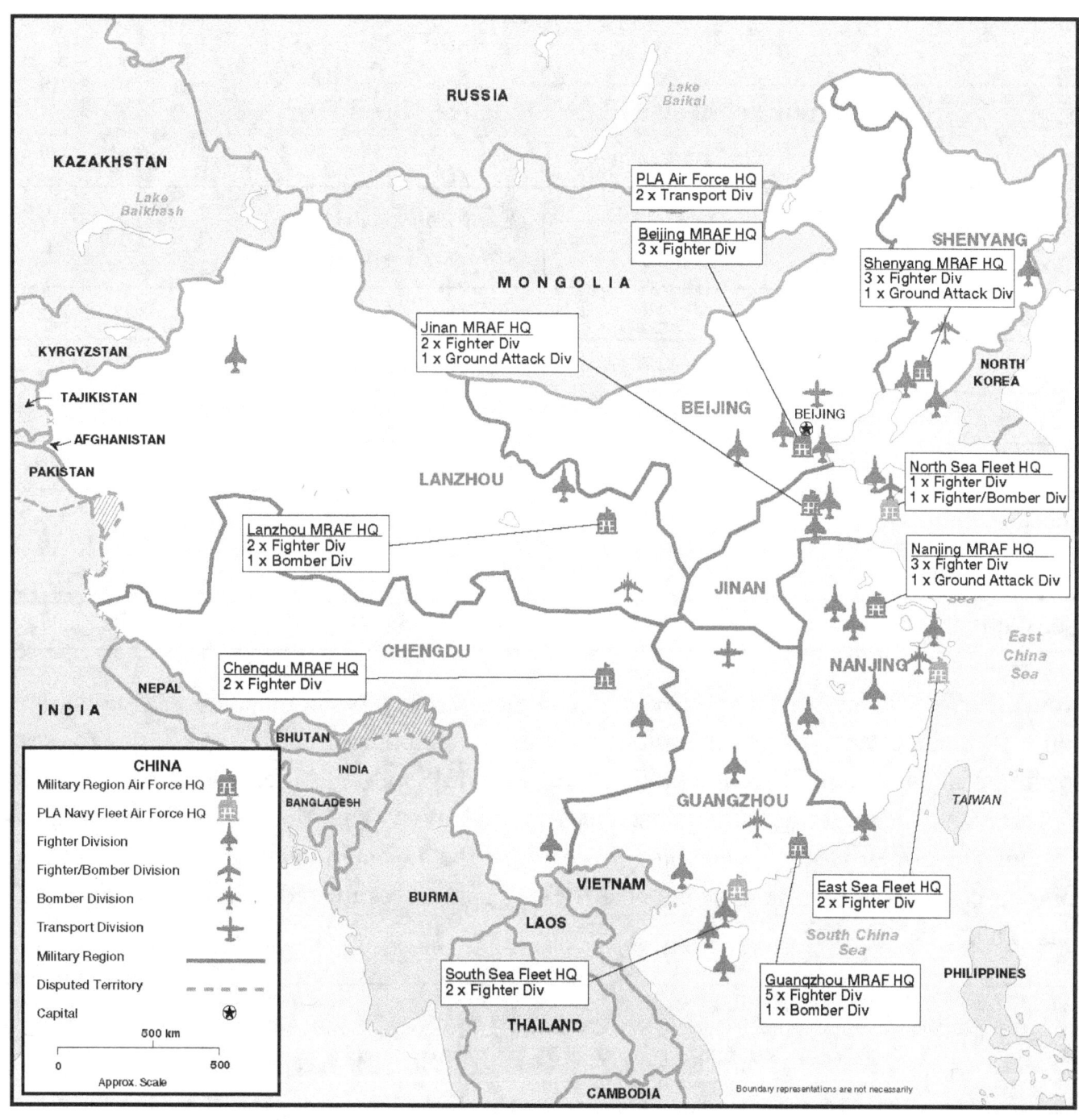

Figure 11. *Major Air Force Units*

Taiwan Strait Military Balance, Naval Forces			
China			Taiwan
	Total	East and South Sea Fleets	Total
Destroyers	25	16	4
Frigates	47	40	22
Tank Landing Ships	25	22	12
Medium Landing Ships	25	20	4
Diesel Submarines	53	28	4
Nuclear Submarines	5	0	0
Coastal Patrol (Missile)	41	34	50

Note: The PLA Navy has a large fleet that includes 72 principal combatants, 58 submarines, some 50 medium and heavy amphibious lift ships, and about 41 coastal missile patrol craft. In the event of a major Taiwan conflict, the East and South Sea Fleets would be expected to participate in direct action against the Taiwan Navy. The North Sea Fleet would be responsible primarily for protecting Beijing and the northern coasts, but could provide mission critical assets to support the other fleets. Taiwan completed delivery of four KIDD-class DDGs in 2006.

Figure 12. *Taiwan Strait Military Balance, Naval Forces*

Figure 13. *Major Naval Units*

China's Missile Forces		
China's Missile Inventory	Launchers/ Missiles	Estimated Range
CSS-4 ICBM	20/20	12,900+ km
CSS-3 ICBM	9-13/16-24	5,470+ km
CSS-2 IRBM	6-10/14-18	2,790+ km
CSS-5 MRBM Mod 1/2	34-38/40-50	1,770+ km
JL-1 SLBM	10-14/10-14	1,770+ km
CSS-6 SRBM	70-80/300-350	600 km
CSS-7 SRBM	110-130/575-625	300 km
JL-2 SLBM	DEVELOPMENTAL	8,000+ km
DF-31 ICBM	INITIAL THREAT AVAILABILITY	7,250+ km
DF-31A ICBM	DEVELOPMENTAL	11,270+ km

Note: China's SRBM force has grown significantly in the past few years. China's Second Artillery maintains at least five operational SRBM brigades; another brigade is deployed with the PLA ground forces garrisoned in the Nanjing Military Region and a second brigade is forming in the Guangzhou Military Region. All of these units are deployed to locations near Taiwan.

Figure 14. *China's Missile Forces*

China's Space Assets	
Inventory	Total
Communications Satellites	14
Navigation Satellites	3
Meteorological Satellites	3
Remote Sensing/Imagery Satellites	6
Scientific Satellites	8
Manned Space System	1
Total	35

Note: China seeks to become a world leader in space development and maintain a leading role in space launch activity. Beijing's goal is to place a satellite into orbit "within hours upon request." With increasingly capable satellites, China is becoming competitive in some markets, but is not yet among the world's technological leaders.

Figure 15. *China's Space Assets*